DRAMATIZED PARODIES
OF
FAMILIAR STORIES

Other books by
Claire Boiko

CHILDREN'S PLAYS FOR CREATIVE ACTORS
PLAYS AND PROGRAMS FOR BOYS AND GIRLS

Dramatized Parodies of Familiar Stories

Six one-act, royalty-free scripts,
with original song lyrics set to well-known melodies,
for performance by young people.

by

CLAIRE BOIKO

Publishers   PLAYS, INC.   *Boston*

[C1980]

Library of Congress Cataloging in Publication Data

Boiko, Claire.
  Dramatized parodies of familiar stories.

  SUMMARY: A collection of plays which give surprising plots and settings to well-known stories and folk tales. Includes production notes.
  1.   Children's plays, American. 2.   Parodies.
[1.   Parodies. 2.   Plays] I.   Title.
PS3552.O55D7 1980   812'.5'4   79-20728
ISBN 0-8238-0240-X

Contents

ROAMIN' JO AND JULI   1
   A lighthearted version of Shakespeare's
   "Romeo and Juliet"

BELINDA AND THE BEAST   27
   A wild-west adventure based on
   "Beauty and the Beast"

ROWDY KATE   57
   A Western "adaptation" of Shakespeare's
   "The Taming of the Shrew"

CYBERNELLA   89
   Space-age disco antics modeled on
   "Cinderella"

THE TOWN THAT COULDN'T WAKE UP   115
   Romantic melodrama that retells
   "Sleeping Beauty"

THE FASTEST THIMBLE IN THE WEST   141
   A new look at
   "The Brave Little Tailor"

DRAMATIZED PARODIES
OF
FAMILIAR STORIES

ROAMIN' JO AND JULI

Roamin' Jo and Juli

*A lighthearted version of
Shakespeare's "Romeo and Juliet"*

Characters

MARSHAL LAWE
WILD BULL MONTANA
ROAMIN' JO MONTANA, *his son*
BEN VOLIO, *Jo's friend*
JULI CHAPLET
MAW CHAPLET
PAW CHAPLET
TIBBLE CHAPLET, *Juli's brother*
JOHN QUINCY PROPER
WORTHINGTON SLIGH
WILLIAM CADWALLADER
MORNINGSTAR, *an Indian*
EIGHT CHAPLET COUSINS, *male and female*

TIME: *The mythical Old West. Sunset, the night of Juli
Chaplet's wedding.*
SETTING: *A square in the town of Verony, Texas. The town
jail is up center. A backless wooden bench is down left,
and up right center are a hitching post and a bed of coals*

3

with a branding iron beside it. A sign hung on a cactus down right points to the Chaplet ranch, and another sign at left points to the Montana ranch.

AT RISE: *Musicians (a guitarist or string band) may sit on apron of stage. An overture of Western songs may be played, then a simple Western tune as* CHAPLET COUSINS, *4 boys and 4 girls, skip on from right, in couples, arm in arm, in time to music. When they reach center, they face the audience, clapping in rhythm to the music.*

COUSINS (*Reciting*):

>Howdy, folks, you're looking well.
>
>Now sit you down and listen a spell,
>
>We turned up the lanterns good and bright,
>
>'Cause a brand-new opry is a-playing here tonight.

1ST COUPLE: Brand-new?

2ND COUPLE: We-e-el, we kinda borrowed some of it from Shorty Shakespeare.

3RD COUPLE: Remember old Shorty Shakespeare, down at the Stratford corral?

4TH COUPLE: But this is our own Western version of *Romeo and Juliet.*

1ST COUPLE: Only we branded it—

COUSINS:

>"Roamin' Jo and Juli" — or
>
>"How the West Was Lost!"

(*Girls curtsy, boys bow.*)

>So, if'n you please —
>
>Unbuckle your six guns,

(*They clap.*)

>Do-si-do,
>
>Remove your Stetsons —

(*The sound of shooting and yelling is heard from off left.*)

And away we go! (*Boys grab girls' hands and all run off right. Shooting and yelling continue off left, and shouting is now heard from off right.* MARSHAL LAWE *enters up center from jail, on the run. He runs left and shouts.*)

MARSHAL: Quiet, you Montanas! I'll put you back in jail! (*There is quiet off left. He runs right.*) Hush up, Chaplets, or I'll fine you another hundred dollars! (*There is quiet off right.* MARSHAL *comes to center and addresses the audience.*) Howdy. I'm the Marshal here. Marshal of Verony, somewhere west of the Pecos. Population — 78, subject to change without notice. As soon as I turn my back, those feuding Montanas and Chaplets will be at it again. The Montanas raise cows, and the Chaplets raise sheep and they both raise Cain! (*Looks left*) Speak of the devil, here comes one of the Montanas now. It's Wild Bull Montana, looking for that no-good son of his, Roamin' Jo Montana. Now, don't you give up on me. I'll think of something to end this feud between the Chaplets and the Montanas or my name isn't Marshal Lawe! (*He opens his coat, revealing an oversized badge, then goes off through the jail.* WILD BULL *and* BEN VOLIO *enter from left.* WILD BULL *flicks his whip in annoyance.*)

WILD BULL: Where is he, Ben? Where's my son, Roamin' Jo? It's time to round up the herd and send the cattle to Abilene. And where's that son of mine? Last year he took off for Californy at roundup time, and the year before it was Mexico.

BEN (*In Spanish accent*): Don't you worry, Señor Montana.

I, Ben Volio, will stay to help with the roundup. You can depend on me. I will be your ever-faithful amigo. (*He puts his hand on* WILD BULL's *shoulder.*)

WILD BULL: Thank you kindly, Ben. I swear, my son Jo doesn't deserve a true-blue friend like you. A rolling tumbleweed, that's what he is. I reckon nothing short of a catastrophe will change that boy. (*"Billy Boy" is played as* ROAMIN' JO *is heard off right, whistling. Music continues under dialogue.*)

BEN (*Cocking his head*): Señor Montana — listen. It sounds like Roamin' Jo. (*He runs up right.*) It is! He's come back. (ROAMIN' JO *enters, knapsack on his back, up right. He throws his arms open.*)

ROAMIN' JO: Paw — Ben — it's me, Roamin' Jo. I'm back! (*Takes off knapsack*)

BEN: Señor Jo! Señor Jo — Sacramento California, but it is good to see you. (*He pumps* JO's *hand enthusiastically.*)

WILD BULL (*Glumly*): Sure, you're back. For how long, Jo? Twenty minutes? Long enough to get your chow?

ROAMIN' JO: No, Paw, I've changed. I'm a new man. I'm here for good.

BEN (*Pleased*): For good! (*To* WILD BULL) Do you hear that, Señor?

WILD BULL (*Turning away stubbornly*): There's nothing on this earth that will keep my son here for good — unless — unless it's a catastrophe.

ROAMIN' JO: But, Paw — I met a gal. I aim to get married.

WILD BULL (*Turning around, astonished*): Married! Well, by jingo, that *is* a catastrophe!

BEN: Ay-yi-yi. Who is she, Señor Jo? A señorita from California?

ROAMIN' JO: She lives closer than that. Matter of fact, she lives right here in Verony. Paw, Ben, she's a hum-dumdinger-ringer. Yahoo! (*He throws his hat in the air, and sings to the tune of "Billy Boy."*)

> I have met myself a gal, yes, indeed, yes, indeed.
>
> There's a gal that's all picked out for this laddie —

BEN (*Singing*):

> Is she pretty?

WILD BULL (*Singing*):

> Who's her maw?

BEN (*Singing*):

> Is she shapely?

WILD BULL (*Singing*):

> Who's her paw?

ROAMIN' JO (*Singing*):

> She is rare,
>
> (*Gazing out dreamily*)
>
> She is fair.

WILD BULL (*Singing*):

> Who *is* her *da-a-ddy?*

ROAMIN' JO (*Singing second verse*):

> She has eyes blueberry bright,
>
> Pretty gal, pretty gal.
>
> Life would be a train to nowhere
>
> Without her.
>
> (*He sighs.*)

BEN (*Singing*):

> Can she cook and can she sew?

ROAMIN' JO (*Singing*):

> Never asked her, I don't know.

WILD BULL (*Singing*):

> Answer me, Jo!
>
> And tell me more about her.

ROAMIN' JO (*Snapping out of his trance*): I told you, Paw, I don't know. I don't know one solitary thing about her.

I saw her down by the creek picking flowers. Well, she just struck me the way lightning strikes a big old oak. (*Going off in a trance*) She set my whole head to buzzing and my ears to tingling, and I declare I don't know if my feet are touching the ground. It's plumb wonderful!

WILD BULL (*Groaning*): I swear, Jo, I don't know which is worse — the way you used to be or the way you are now. Either way, you're no use to me for rounding up the cattle. (*To* BEN, *confidentially*) Ben, I want you to stick close to Roamin' Jo. He's a mite soft in the head. See if you can't talk some sense to him — and find out about this gal.

BEN: Si, Señor. I will guard him with my life.

WILD BULL: All right now, Jo. I'm going down to the corral. You and Ben come down when you're ready. Jo? (*Jo sits on bench down left, a foolish grin on his face.* WILD BULL *snaps his fingers in* JO's *face.* JO *doesn't change his expression.*) Jo? Whew. (*Aside*) She must be some gal to do this to Jo. (*He walks left*) Who could she be? Annabelle? Betsy Mae? Cassie Lou? (*He exits still counting off names*) Dorinda? (*As* WILD BULL *exits left,* JULI CHAPLET *enters right, looking up at sky. She does not notice* JO *or* BEN.)

MAW CHAPLET (*Entering*): Juli? Juli? Where are you, Juli?

JULI: Right here, Maw. Just taking a walk.

MAW: Don't you stray too far.

JULI: I won't, Maw. (MAW *exits.* JULI *goes down center and looks up.*) Look there. The stars are coming out like a field of daisies upside down.

ROAMIN' JO (*Gripping* BEN's *arm*): Look, Ben. That gal. That's her. That's the gal I love.

BEN (*Alarmed*): *That* señorita? Oh, no, not *that* señorita. Ay-yi-yi-Acapulco! Don't you know who she is?

ROAMIN' JO: Shush, Ben. She's saying something to the

stars. Listen. (*"Aura Lee" is played softly behind* JULI*'s speech.*)

JULI: Listen to me, stars. Listen to me because there's no one in this wicked world I can talk to but you. (*She puts her hand on her cheek and sighs.*)

ROAMIN' JOE: She's sighing. I wonder what ails the poor thing. Aw — look at that, Ben. She's putting her little old hand on her little old cheek. I wish I were that little old hand.

JULI: Do you know what, stars? This here is my wedding night. My folks are marrying me off to a dude from St. Louis. Isn't that a sin and a shame, stars? I can't love a dude I never even curtsied to before. Besides, I'm waiting for somebody else. A feller on a big white horse with a golden saddle and silver spurs. I saw him 'way off in the distance today. Wish I knew who he was. Wish he'd come soon. (*Singing to tune of "Aura Lee"*)

There's mystery where the twilight fades,
There's strangeness in the air,
My own true love he awaits for me,
Out in the great Somewhere —
Somewhere near, somewhere far,
Like a guessing game,
Unknown, unknown, true love my own,
I wait to hear your name.

MAW (*Re-entering*): Juli! Juli! We're almost ready to start the wedding ceremony.

JULI (*Reluctantly*): I'm coming, Maw. (*Looks up again*) Goodnight, stars. Next time you see me, I'll be married to a stranger I don't love. (*She wipes her eyes and goes slowly off right with* MAW.)

ROAMIN' JO: Wait! (BEN *pins* JO*'s arms so he can't follow* JULI.)

BEN: No, Señor Jo. You mustn't.

ROAMIN' JO: Let go of me, Ben. (BEN *lets go.*) Didn't you hear that gal? She has to marry somebody she doesn't love. And didn't you hear her asking for the feller on the white horse? There's only one feller in the world like that — me!

BEN: You must not get mixed up with her. Please come away. I tell you, the señorita is not for you.

ROAMIN' JO: And I tell you she is the *only* gal for me. Why (*He straightens and puts his hand on his heart solemnly.*), I would rather die than be without her.

BEN: You will die even quicker if you are with her. Señor Jo — that is *Juli Chaplet.*

ROAMIN' JO (*Astonished*): Juli Chaplet! *Juli Chaplet!* Great guns, I *have* been away a long spell. Last time I saw little Juli she was a slip of nothing in pigtails. (*He shakes his head.*) A Chaplet. I went and fell in love with a Chaplet. (*Resolutely*) By doggies, Ben, I don't care a hoot. I don't care who her family is. That gal is mine! (*He grabs* BEN *and twirls him around square-dance fashion, singing to the tune of "Billy Boy."*)

I'll be meeting you right soon, Juli gal, Juli gal.

I'll be meeting you real soon, dear Miss Juli.

(*Stops singing*) Come on, Ben. Let's go help Paw a spell, and then — I have plans! (*He pulls* BEN *off left with a whoop, taking knapsack with him.* MARSHAL LAWE *enters from jail, shaking his head, and comes down center.*)

MARSHAL LAWE: Trouble. T-r-o-u-b-l-e. I smell trouble in the wind, as sure as you're born. And you know what trouble smells like — gunsmoke. (*"She'll Be Coming 'Round the Mountain" is playing under dialogue.*) Oh-oh. I hear the Chaplets coming. Well, I'd best round up any stray Montanas that might want to make trouble.

(*He exits left as* MAW *and* PAW CHAPLET, JULI *and* MORNINGSTAR *enter right.*)

MAW: This is going to be a grand night for you Juli. We'll have us a big barbecue, and then your own beautiful wedding.

JULI (*Sitting on bench, head in her hands*): Yes'm, I reckon so. (MAW *sits beside her.* PAW *stands by bench.* MORNINGSTAR *stands down right with folded arms, Indian fashion.*)

PAW: What now, Juli. What ails you?

JULI: Well, Paw, I have a right to look poorly. I don't like the way you engaged me. Did you have to order a man from the Sears, Roebuck catalogue?

PAW: Juli, we explained that a hundred times —

MAW: Hush, Paw. You have to be firm with Juli. Now, Juli, there's nobody hereabouts fitten to marry with anymore. The only feller left is that rascal Roamin' Jo. And he's a — a — Montana.

PAW: Sooner have you marry a Yankee than a Montana!

JULI (*With spunk*): How does everybody know Roamin' Jo is a rascal? Nobody's seen him for years. He's been in California.

MAW: Never you mind. I heard about him from Miz Ordway, who heard it from Jenny Zoriah, who heard it from the sister-in-law of the Montanas' cook. If'n *they* say he's a rascal, it must be so.

PAW: Stop all this talk about the Montanas and get on with the wedding. Look at the sky. It's after sundown. Your brother Tibble should be bringing the bridegroom from the station soon. Cheer up, Juli. Your bridegroom is a real fancy feller.

MAW: Let me tell her, Paw. You know what the catalogue said? It said that Mr. John Quincy Proper —

PAW: That's the feller's name — John Quincy Proper.

MAW: Shush, Paw. Anyhow, he's very well-to-do. He has his own marrying suit and he will bring his own witnesses and a legal type of marrying paper good in the United States *and* Canada.

PAW: Shucks, Juli, you're going on sixteen — remember that's a mite old for some fellers, but Mr. Proper didn't say boo when we wrote him that you were just a little overage. (*"She'll Be Coming 'Round the Mountain" is played very fast.*)

TIBBLE (*Entering right, followed by* PROPER, SLIGH *and* CADWALLADER): Here we are, Maw. I brought the bridegroom and the witnesses from the station. (MAW *starts toward* TIBBLE, *who begins to sidle left.*) Can I go, Maw? Please, Maw? (MAW *follows him suspiciously, as* PROPER *and others stand stiff and pompous up right.*)

MAW (*Collaring him*): Hold on a piece, son Tibble. Where do you figure on going? We're about to commence the weddin' barbecue.

TIBBLE (*Sneakily*): Shucks, Maw. I just thought I'd fool around the creek — maybe catch a couple of fish.

MAW: A couple of fish, eh? A couple of fish named Montana, maybe?

PAW: Don't you start any trouble, Tibble. If trouble comes, let it be on their heads.

MAW: You get along home, Tibble. (*Pointing right*) That-a-way. Get all the gal cousins together, and find some nice boy cousins to dance with them.

TIBBLE: Boy cousins? We got us a passel of cousins. I don't know one from the other, Maw.

MAW: You don't have to. Just look them square in the eye. If they look like fresh-faced, clean-cut, up-and-coming, ginger-peachy fellers, they're just natcherly Chaplet boy cousins. Now scat. We want to introduce Juli to her fiancy. (TIBBLE *runs off right.* PROPER *comes down center, bows first to* MAW, *then to* JULI.)

PROPER: Good evening, dear ladies. You must be the happy Chaplet family. I am your friendly bridegroom, John Quincy Proper. (*He bows, leans down and kisses* JULI*'s hand.*) And this must be the blushing bride —

JULI (*Horrified*): Maw, help! He's trying to bite my hand! (*She snatches her hand away.*)

MAW: Don't be a-feared, Juli. That's just one of those foreign customs. He's looking your hand over to see if you have all your fingers.

PROPER: Heh, heh. Precious. She's just precious! Rather small, but then, good things come in small packages, eh? (*JULI gets off the bench and scuttles over to* MAW. *She hunches down to appear even smaller.*)

JULI: I'm awful small. Maybe I'm too small to suit you. (*MAW pushes her forward firmly.*)

MAW: Be quiet, Juli. (*To* PROPER) She's small, but she's strong. Strong as a mule. (*JULI coughs.* MAW *puts her hand over* JULI*'s mouth.*) Healthy, too. Never had a sick day in her life.

PROPER: Splendid. She'll do nicely. Now, let me introduce the witnesses, Mr. Worthington Sligh and Mr. William Cadwallader.

ALL: Howdy.

SLIGH *and* CADWALLADER (*Removing their hats in unison*): Howdy.

CADWALLADER: Delighted to be here.

SLIGH: I just natcherly love weddings.

PROPER: Now, if you don't mind, there is just one little trifling legal paper for you to sign before we commence the wedding. (*He holds out a paper and* SLIGH *presents pen.*)

JULI: Wait a minute. What's it say? What's that paper say?

PROPER (*With a wink to the witnesses*): Why, it simply states that Mr. Proper, Mr. Sligh and Mr. Cadwallader arrived at your ranch safely. Here you are. The pen has fresh ink, the document is ready, and the time is now! (*Pitch is given immediately, then "She'll Be Coming 'Round the Mountain" is played, as* PROPER, SLIGH *and* CADWALLADER *speak, rather than sing, in rhythm to the accompaniment.*)

    You must sign upon this line — (*Giving paper and pen to* PAW, *who signs*)

SLIGH:

    On the line —

CADWALLADER:

    That's just fine!

PROPER (*Handing paper to* MAW, *who signs*):

    Put your mark upon this spot —

SLIGH:

    That's the plot —

CADWALLADER:

    Thanks a lot!

PROPER (*Guiding* JULI*'s hand as she signs*):

    Your John Hancock on the paper —

SLIGH:

    Will end this little caper —

CADWALLADER:

    Everything will be shipshaper —

SLIGH, PROPER *and* CADWALLADER (*Together*):

    That's the plan. That's the plan.

PROPER: Thanks a lot! (*Whisks paper away and puts it into pocket*) Done! Signed, sealed, and dee-livered. Now all we need is a wedding ceremony to make things legal.

MAW (*Joyfully*): A wedding ceremony. Yes-siree-bob. But first, we're going to have us a barbecue and square dance. And look there — yonder come the boys and gals!

(*"Buffalo Gals" is played as* CHAPLET COUSINS *enter right, skipping, arm in arm, and line up at front of stage. Each carries two large cooking spoons. Others move upstage to make room for* COUSINS.)

COUSINS (*Singing to the tune of "Buffalo Gals"*):

We're having ourselves a barbecue, barbecue, barbecue
(*Tap spoons together*)
With chops 'n' mutton, 'n' good lamb stew,
(*Tap spoons*)
Bring a hearty appetite!
(*Tap partners' spoons*)
O, come along now and join the boss,
(*Tap spoons*)
A couple more won't make us cross,
(*Tap spoons*)
Just bring along your barbecue sauce,
(*Tap spoons*)
There's a party here tonight!
(*Tap partners' spoons*)
Yahoo!
(*They skip back three steps, shake spoons.* COUSINS *and others hold a pose.* ROAMIN' JO *and* BEN *enter down left.*)

ROAMIN' JO: Look at that, Ben. Big doings.

BEN: Come away from here, Señor Jo. These are Chaplet hombres. Come away, please, before they shoot us dead.
(TIBBLE *sneaks in left behind them and grabs them by the collars.*)

TIBBLE (*Triumphantly*): Aha, I gotcha.

JO *and* BEN (*Hands in the air; together*): We surrender.

TIBBLE (*Grinning*): Sure you do. Nobody can hold out when they see all those pretty gals at our barbecue. Howdy, cousins.

JO *and* BEN (*Together*): Cousins?

TIBBLE: Sure. Aren't you fresh-faced, clean-cut, up-and-coming, ginger-peachy fellers?

Jo *and* BEN (*Nodding; together*): Natcherly.

TIBBLE: Then you must be Chaplets and cousins of Miss Juli and me.

Jo: Miss Juli — is she here?

TIBBLE: In the flesh.

ROAMIN' Jo: And you say we — er — cousins are invited to the barbecue?

TIBBLE: That's the idea.

ROAMIN' Jo: We accept. Shake, cousin! (*He pumps* TIBBLE*'s hand.*)

BEN (*Hiding his eyes*): Oh-h-h! Tabasco! Tamales! Tortillas and frijoles!

MAW (*Coming down right*): Well, now, don't just stand there like a passel of fence posts. Come on, boys and gals! Play those guitars. Get a partner, everybody dance. (COUSINS *form a square dance set at center.* JULI *and* MAW *sit on bench down left, with* PAW *and* TIBBLE *kneeling in front of it.* MORNINGSTAR *stands beside* JULI. PROPER, SLIGH, *and* CADWALLADER *stand behind bench and* Jo *and* BEN *sit on stage down left. Appropriate square dance music is played, and a caller may call a square dance. At the end of the dance,* COUSINS *hold the square.*)

PAW (*Standing, as all applaud dancers*): Come on, everybody. There's food a-plenty at the Chaplet ranch. Let's eat! (*All shout approval and* COUSINS *exit first, arm in arm, up right.* TIBBLE *runs off right, whooping.* MAW *and* PAW *usher* PROPER, SLIGH, *and* CADWALLADER *off right.* Jo *takes* JULI *by the arm before she can leave and brings her to center.* BEN *tags along beside* Jo, *and* MORNINGSTAR *stays close to* JULI.)

ROAMIN' JO: Miss Juli, ma'am, may I speak to you?

JULI (*Smiling*): Oh, you must be a boy cousin. Of course you can speak to me. (BEN *nudges* JO. MORNINGSTAR *folds her arms and stands close to* JULI. JO *looks at them, annoyed.*)

ROAMIN' JO: Say, look here, you two. Two's company, four's a stampede. Go on about your business.

MORNINGSTAR: I no leave Miss Juli. Mother speak, say I keep eye on Miss Juli.

JULI: Now, Morningstar, Maw said you were to keep an eye on me. She didn't say anything about your ears. Just trot over yonder. (MORNINGSTAR *reluctantly goes down right.*)

ROAMIN' JO: You heard the lady, Ben. Vamoose. (*He shoos* BEN *up left with his hat.*)

BEN: Ay-yi-yi, I will be sorry. (MORNINGSTAR *and* BEN *keep moving slowly closer to their charges as the conversation continues.* JULI *sits on the bench.* JO *puts one foot on the bench, and holds his hat on his chest, respectfully.*)

ROAMIN' JO: Miss Juli, I've been admiring you from afar, and I want you to know my intentions are strictly honorable.

JULI: Why, thank you. I appreciate hearing about your intentions, but it's too late. I've been spoken for.

ROAMIN' JO: I know, I know. But Miss Juli, forgive my saying so, but it doesn't seem as if you care a heap for that dude.

JULI (*Looking around cautiously before confiding in* JO): Well, you do have sharp eyes. It's true. I can't seem to cotton to that Mr. Proper. He isn't what he seems to be. (*Smiling at* JO) But you, now. I knew the minute I saw that honest, clean cut, ginger-peachy face — why, you're just as honest as the day is long.

ROAMIN' JO (*To audience*): Oh, the days are a-getting short-
er! (To JULI) Miss Juli, you make me ashamed. Fact of
the matter is, I'm no better than that dude. (BEN *begins
to move in with purpose.*) I'm not what I seem to be,
either — (BEN *covers* JO*'s face with his sombrero.*)

BEN: He talks too much, Señorita. Let's go home, Señor.

ROAMIN' JO (*Pushing the hat away*): No, I have to tell her,
Ben. (*He stands, bravely.*) My conscience would plague
me until doomsday if I lied to you. Miss Juli. I am — I
am Roamin' Jo Montana.

JULI: Roamin' Jo Montana! I don't believe it!

MORNINGSTAR (*Grabbing* JULI *and pulling her right*):
Roamin' Jo Montana! I believe it. Ugh! Bad medicine.
We go. Ugh!

JULI (*As she is pulled off right*): Wait —

BEN (*Pushing* JO *left with determination*): No more of this,
Señor. The Chaplets will come back with guns and a
posse.

ROAMIN' JO: I'll go for now, Ben. But I'll think of a way to
save that gal from that dude. I've *got* to! (*As they exit
left,* PROPER, SLIGH, *and* CADWALLADER *enter right, and
come down center.*)

PROPER: Are we alone? (SLIGH *and* CADWALLADER *look
around, then nod.*) Good. Now listen, you two. We have
a scheme to dream!

SLIGH: Right, Dude. I just naturally love schemes.

CADWALLADER (*Sitting on bench*): Hey, Dude, do you figure we have the Chaplets fooled?

PROPER (*Coming to bench*): Certainly, Cad. They are as
innocent as woolly little lambs. And what do we do to
woolly little lambs?

SLIGH *and* CADWALLADER (*Together*): We fleece 'em.

PROPER: Precisely. Heh, heh. Who would guess that we

waylaid the *real* bridegroom in the train? Gentlemen (*He doffs his hat*) — meet Dick Red-Eye, the Deadly Dude.

SLIGH: I just naturally love dudes. Meet Sneaky Pete — the loudest gun in the West. (*Lifts hat*)

CADWALLADER: Pleased to make your acquaintance. I'm Billy the Cad myself, the lovingest-leavingest cad in the West.

PROPER: Enough, enough. Now, listen. As soon as I have married Juli, the entire Chaplet ranch will be mine. Those fools signed their entire ranch over to me when they signed that "trifling little paper." Heh, heh. Now, let's get those sheep-raising fools together and get this wedding under way. (*They exit down right, as* JULI *and* MORNINGSTAR *enter from up right.* JULI *wipes her eyes as* MORNINGSTAR *holds out white veil.*)

MORNINGSTAR: Please, Miss Juli. You try on wedding veil.

JULI: I have no heart for it, Morningstar. Oh, Morningstar — I've only known Jo an hour and I *love* him. I love a *Montana.* Why can't he have some other name — Smith or Jones, or even Terwilliger? What's a name, anyhow? Shucks, a rose would smell just as pretty if you called it a cactus. (*She sits on bench.* ROAMIN' JO *enters down left, motioning* BEN *to come on. He drops to his knees before* JULI, *who draws back startled.*) Oh, Roamin' Jo, go back. If my brother Tibble should find you here, he'd shoot you first and think about it afterward. (*"Shenandoah" is playing softly as* JO *takes* JULI*'s hand.*)

ROAMIN' JO: Miss Juli, listen a minute. I can't let you waste your life with that dude Proper, and I can't bear the thought of spending my life away from you. (*Sings to tune of "Shenandoah"*)

Miss Juli, gal, I long to see you,
Long to be your own true lover.

Miss Juli, gal, I long to free you,
To bring a dawning day
From your night of sorrow.
Miss Juli, gal, I'm pledged to serve you,
Oh, I swear it, by the moon.
Miss Juli, gal, we're leaving soon,
Away, we're bound away,
To a bright tomorrow.

(*He pulls her to her feet, and they start left.*) Come away, Juli — now. (*As they walk left,* TIBBLE *jumps onstage from up left, with two six-guns in his hands.*)

TIBBLE: Stop! Stop dead in your tracks. I heard every word, Montana! (JULI *rushes to* TIBBLE, *who brushes her aside.*)

JULI: Tibble, put away those guns.

TIBBLE: Hush up, Juli. Listen, Montana. You can't come sneak-wheedling around my little sister. For that I am entitled to fill you full of lead until you shake like a rattle full of pumpkin seeds.

ROAMIN' JO: Stand aside, Tibble. I aim to make Juli my wife.

TIBBLE: I'll see you dead first. Ten paces, Montana.

ROAMIN' JO: Ten paces, Chaplet. (*They stand back to back for the shootdown, then count as they step off distance.*)

TIBBLE *and* JO: One . . . two . . . three . . . four . . . five . . . (BEN *steps in front of* JO.)

BEN: Stop. I will do the shooting. Give me your guns, Señor Jo.

ROAMIN' JO (*Pushing him aside*): There's only one way to deal with this galoot. Stand aside. Where were we?

TIBBLE: Five.

TIBBLE *and* JO: Five . . . six . . . seven . . . eight . . . nine — (*As both turn,* MARSHAL LAWE, *followed by* PAW *and*

WILD BULL, *runs in from center and steps between them.*)

MARSHAL LAWE: Stop, stop in the name of the law. Marshal Lawe, that is. (*To audience*) You folks recollect I said I'd find something to stop this feuding? Well, I have. (*To others*) Men, your Uncle Sam sends you greetings.

ALL: Greetings?

MARSHAL LAWE: There has been an uprising in the Dakotas. General Custer needs every able-bodied man in these parts to go and fight in the United States Cavalry.

ALL: The United States Cavalry!

MARSHAL LAWE: All right. Line up, you new recruits. (*He lines up* TIBBLE, JO, WILD BULL, BEN *and* PAW) Stomachs in, and chins out. March yourselves down to the county courthouse so's I can swear you in and give you your beautiful new uniforms. Right face. Hup, two, three, four. Left, right, left. Forward, march! (*They march off up left as* MAW *comes running in right, followed by* PROPER, SLIGH *and* CADWALLADER.)

MAW (*Calling after them*): Paw, don't forget your galoshes when it rains, and put on your red flannels when it snows. Tibble, mind your manners.

JULI (*Going to* MAW *and crying on her shoulder*): Oh, Maw, it's terrible. He's gone out of my life.

MAW: There, there, Juli. (*She brings her down to bench, and they sit.* MORNINGSTAR *stands close by.*) Don't fret. I'll write to Washington and tell them Paw is needed for the sheep-shearing. Tibble, too.

JULI: But, Maw, it isn't just Paw and Tibble. It's Roamin' Jo Montana. I love him. Indeed I do.

MAW: What? You love a *Montana?* How could you, Juli Chaplet? Why, you're engaged to this fine upstanding Mr. Proper.

JULI: Upstanding, is he? I didn't see him and his witnesses

marching off to help General Custer. (PROPER *comes right of bench. He bows.*)

PROPER: Ah, Miss Juli. How could I leave you and your helpless little mother in this wilderness? Besides, this is my wedding day. Right, gentlemen?

SLIGH *and* CADWALLADER (*Together*): Right!

MAW: Shucks, the excitement put the wedding clear out of my head. Paw was supposed to fetch Preacher Lawrence from the next town.

PROPER: Never mind. Cadwallader can marry us. He was a licensed notary public before he turned to more profitable ventures.

CADWALLADER: I'll get out my book of ceremonies.

JULI: Maw, Mr. Proper, gents. I can't go any further. 'Twouldn't be honorable. (*She stands, with her hand on her heart.*) I love another, Mr. Proper. Roamin' Jo Montana. I want to marry him. Thank you kindly for thinking of me, but no other feller will do.

PROPER (*Snarling*): Why, you stubborn little fool! Pete — Billy — grab her maw. (*Pointing to pit and post, up center*) Tie her to the hitching post next to that branding pit yonder. You, Injun gal, fan that flame. (MORNINGSTAR *goes to pit, stands with arms folded.*)

MAW: What? Don't you touch me! (SLIGH *and* CADWALLADER *drag* MAW *to the pit and tie her to post.*)

JULI: Mr. Proper! This is *not proper!*

PROPER (*Sneering*): Heh, heh. I am not your pious Mr. Proper, my dear. We took care of him on the train. I am Dick Red-Eye.

MAW (*In terror*): The Deadly Dude! All is lost.

PROPER: Heat up the branding iron, Billy. (SLIGH *holds the iron over the fire.*) Now Miss Persnickety — are you ready, willing and able? (*He takes* JULI *firmly by arm.*)

CADWALLADER (*Taking book from pocket*): *I'm* ready, willing, and able. (*Reading*) Ladies and gents of the jury, we are gathered to hang this here varmint —

PROPER: Turn to the *wedding* ceremony, you idiot! The short version.

JULI (*Struggling*): I'll never marry you!

MAW: That's my girl. Why, I'd a heap rather you married Roamin' Jo than this high-living, card-playing fancy Dan.

PROPER: Very noble. You, Injun, *fan,* I said. (MORNING-STAR *takes her blanket off and fans as if making smoke signals.*) Pick up that brand, Pete. Is it ready?

SLIGH: Red-hot and sizzling, boss. I just natcherly love branding!

PROPER: Good. Miss Juli, marry me — or I'll barbecue your maw!

JULI: Don't you dare! Stop. Stop, I beg you. I'll do anything you say. I'll even marry you. Only don't hurt my maw.

CADWALLADER: Ahem. (*Reading*) Be it hereby known that these goods are placed on the block for auction —

PROPER: Find the wedding ceremony, you numskull.

CADWALLADER: Sure, boss. (*Flips pages of book*) Right away. Ahem. Here it is. Join hands. (PROPER *grabs* JULI's *hand as* CADWALLADER *reads.*) Do you, Dick Red-Eye, take this here woman to be your lawful wedded wife?

PROPER: I do. I certainly do.

CADWALLADER: And do you, Juli Chaplet, take this here man to be your lawful wedded husband?

JULI: I — I — (SLIGH *moves the brand over* MAW's *head threateningly.*) I do.

CADWALLADER: Then I now pronounce you — (*He turns the page.*) judge and jury!

PROPER: Man and wife, you blockhead. Hurry.

CADWALLADER (*Turning page back*): That's right. I now pronounce you man and — (MARSHAL LAWE *enters up center.* WILD BULL, JO *and* BEN, *with rifles, enter from down left.* PAW *and* TIBBLE *enter from down right, with rifles. All wear Cavalry hats and scarves. They surround* PROPER.)

MARSHAL LAWE: Stop! I now pronounce you prisoners of the United States Cavalry. Untie that woman, you varmints. (SLIGH *hastily unties* MAW. PROPER, SLIGH *and* CADWALLADER *put their hands up.*)

MAW: Paw, you came back! How did you know we were in trouble? (PAW *brings* MORNINGSTAR *to center.*)

PAW: Our own Morningstar saved you. (*She hangs her head modestly.*) She sent up smoke signals from yonder branding pit. The Marshal saw them, and back we all came before you could say "Sitting Bull."

MAW: I say we give three cheers for Morningstar!

ALL: Hip-hip-hooray! Hip-hip-hooray! Hip-hip-hooray!

MORNINGSTAR (*Holding up hand in Indian greeting*): Ugh. It was no heap big deed. Any red-blooded Indian maiden do same thing.

MARSHAL LAWE: Tibble, take those outlaws to the jail and lock them up for the night. (TIBBLE *motions the villains up center.*)

PROPER: Curses, foiled again! (*They exit into jail with* TIBBLE.)

PAW: And now it's time to start up the wedding again.

MAW: The wedding? Whose wedding? Now, Paw, let me handle this.

PAW: I'll give the orders now, Maw. The army made a man of me! Everyone is invited to the wedding of these star-crossed-up lovers. (*He joins* JO *and* JULI's *hands. They pose at center, with* PAW *in middle holding his hand over theirs.*) Roamin' Jo and Juli!

ALL: Hooray! (*They gather around couple and* PAW. *"Buffalo Gals" is played as* COUSINS *enter and form a horseshoe in back of* JO, JULI, *and* PAW. COUSINS *carry jingle bells which they shake in time to the music. All sing to the tune of "Buffalo Gals"*)

> We're having ourselves a wedding today,
> Wedding today, wedding today,
> So dance 'n' frolic, 'n' all sashay,
> In honor of Jo and Juli.
> There never was such a loving pair,
> Loving pair, loving pair,
> There's nobody like them anywhere,
> They love each other truly!
> (*Curtain begins to close.*)
> They love each other truly!
> (*All cheer.*)

TIBBLE (*Re-entering from jail, firing cap guns*): Yippee! (*Curtain*)

THE END

Roamin' Jo and Juli

PRODUCTION NOTES

Characters: 13 male; 7 female; as many extras as desired for other Chaplets and Montanas.

Playing Time: 40 minutes.

Costumes; Western dress. Marshal Lawe has an oversized badge on his vest, under his coat, and wears a white Stetson and six-guns. Maw wears long dress with apron and a shawl. Juli is dressed in white. Morningstar wears Indian dress, and has an Indian blanket around her shoulders. Proper and witnesses are dressed in black. Proper has a top hat, cape, and cane. Ben wears Spanish dress: white ruffled shirt, sombrero, serape, etc. Other men wear jeans and colorful shirts. Jo and Tibble wear six-guns. At the end of play, the men put on Cavalry hats and yellow Cavalry scarves, and carry rifles.

Properties: Whip; knapsack; document; pen; 16 large cooking spoons; wedding veil; book; prop rifles and six-guns; jingle bells.

Setting: A square in the town of Verony, Texas. The town jail is up center. Other stores (barbershop, feed stores, hotel with swinging doors) may be right and left. Up center are a hitching post with a rope attached, and a bed of coals with a branding iron beside it. A backless wooden bench is placed down left, near a cactus with a sign hanging on it: BEWARE — MONTANA RANCH THAT-A-WAY. Another cactus down right has a sign: KEEP OFF — CHAPLET RANCH THIS-A-WAY. Exits are up and down right and left, and through jail at center.

Lighting: No special effects.

Sound: Offstage shooting and yelling, as indicated in text. Musicians may accompany singers, or recorded accompaniment may be played offstage. Musicians (guitarist or band made up of guitar, banjo, jug, washboard, etc.) may sit on apron of stage or on auditorium floor. A square dance record with caller may be used for dance, or musicians may accompany dancers. Play may also be easily adapted for performance without music.

BELINDA AND THE BEAST

Belinda and the Beast

*A wild-west adventure
based on "Beauty and the Beast"*

Characters

JIMMY TONSILS, *singing cowboy*
HU HEE, *Confucius of the sagebrush*
CHICKEN-FEATHER, *Indian not-so-brave*
CAPTAIN ABLE MCREADY, *Cavalry officer*
TROOPER HENRY HOOPER, *lovelorn corporal*
ABIGAIL HUCKLEBERRY, *lovelorn prairie flower*
BURRITO, *appealing boy waif*
SASSAFRAS, *appealing girl waif*
B.J. BEAST, *incredible hunk and scourge of the West*
VARMINT ⎰ *double trouble, henchmen of the Beast*
VIPER ⎱
BUCK BUCKTHORNE, *wealthy rancher*
BELINDA BUCKTHORNE, *beautiful heroine*
MRS. POMPOSIA SMYTHE-SMITHERS, *a scheming, wicked
   woman*
FASTIDIA ⎰ *her persnickety daughters*
GAUDIA ⎱
PARSON WORTHY, *bemused man of the cloth*
FOUR BADMEN
FOUR COWBOYS AND FOUR GALS

29

Scene 1

Time: *When the West was young.*

Setting: *No-Man's-Land, in the Badlands of the Southwest.*

Before Rise: *This scene is played before the curtain. At center is a pole with sign reading,* no-man's-land. no woman's neither. beware of beast. *There is a large rock at right. At left is a water tower.* Hu Hee *stands on steps of water tower, holding small gong and striker. He looks offstage, shading eyes with hand.* Jimmy Tonsils, *holding guitar, enters and addresses audience.*

Jimmy (*To audience*): Howdy. They call me Jimmy Tonsils, the wanderin' song and dance man. (*Singing to tune of "Down in the Valley"*)

> Oh, I'm a lone cowboy,
> A-traveling' far,
> Up highways and byways,
> With my guitar.

(*Pointing to sign; speaking*) See that sign? That's new in this territory. Used to be nice and peaceable hereabouts. Then the Beast came. (*Sings to tune of "Down in the Valley"*)

> The Beast came from nowhere
> Gobblin' towns one by one,
> With hordes of bad hombres,
> Like Attila the Hun.

(*Speaking*) Nobody has ever seen Mr. B. J. Beast, but they say that when he comes near, strong men quiver, women quail, and even fearless Injuns faint dead away.

Hu Hee (*Pointing; excitedly*): Ah, so. In far distance, see cloud of suspicious dust. (*Beats gong*) Beast alert! Beast alert! First-stage Beast alert!

JIMMY TONSILS (*Alarmed*): Yikes! Thanks for the warning, Hu Hee. I'm going to make myself scarce. (*He exits, as* CHICKEN FEATHER *enters through center curtain on hands and knees. He stands, wets finger and holds it up to wind, then hoots three times.* CAPTAIN MCREADY *enters, followed by* TROOPER HOOPER, *holding bouquet of flowers, and* ABIGAIL.)

MCREADY: Thanks, Chicken Feather.

HU HEE (*Turning; surprised*): Captain McReady! First-stage Beast alert in progress. You have perhaps two minutes of safety.

MCREADY: Not much time for a marriage proposal. (*To* HOOPER) Hurry, Trooper Hooper. Chicken Feather and I will protect you from the Beast.

HOOPER: Thank you, sir. That blasted Beast has interrupted us every time I've tried to pop the question to Miss Abigail. (HOOPER *offers flowers to* ABIGAIL. *She accepts them shyly.* MCREADY, CHICKEN FEATHER *and* HU HEE *watch with interest.*) Ahem, ahem.

MCREADY: Go on!

HU HEE: Time running out. Beast come soon.

CHICKEN FEATHER (*Wetting finger, holding it up to wind*): Beast come *very* soon.

HOOPER: I didn't expect an audience.

MCREADY (*Bawling an order to* CHICKEN FEATHER *and* HU HEE): About — face! (*They both turn, then* MCREADY *turns. Sound of hoofbeats is heard from offstage.*)

ABIGAIL: Was that an earthquake or a *beastquake?*

MCREADY: Hurry, Henry. Propose! Before it's too late! (*Sound of hoofbeats gets louder.* HU HEE *points excitedly offstage.*)

HU HEE (*Thumping gong*): Second stage! Head for hills!

The Beast! The Beast! (HOOPER *begins to usher* ABIGAIL *hurriedly off.*)

HOOPER: I'm sorry, Miss Abigail. No proposal today.

ABIGAIL (*Wailing*): Oh, Henry. Shall we ever wed? (HENRY *and* ABIGAIL *rush off right.* HU HEE *climbs down ladder, running to* MCREADY *and* CHICKEN FEATHER, *and beating gong rapidly.*)

HU HEE: Run! Run! Run for honorable lives! (*He exits, center.*)

MCREADY (*Nervously*): Did you hear that, Chicken Feather? The Beast is coming! (CHICKEN FEATHER *faints.* MCREADY *catches him.*) Sound the retreat! March to the rear! (*He backs off right, dragging* CHICKEN FEATHER, *as sound of hoofbeats grows louder.* BELINDA BUCKTHORNE *runs on, left, followed by* BURRITO *and* SASSAFRAS, *howling in fear.* BELINDA *clutches a book.*)

BELINDA: Hurry, children. The Beast's henchmen are directly behind us!

SASSAFRAS: Miss Belinda, they snatched the picnic basket right out of my *hands.* (*She bawls.*)

BURRITO: Señorita Belinda, I am so afraid. I have heard that the Beast is twelve feet tall and covered with green hair like Spanish moss!

BELINDA: There, there, children. Don't worry. (*They stop, center.*) I will protect you. (VIPER *and* VARMINT *run in, left.* VARMINT *carries flag with skull and crossbones.* VIPER *holds picnic basket, and gun, which he shoots into air.* BURRITO *and* SASSAFRAS *scream and cower behind* BELINDA, *who faces the outlaws bravely.*)

VARMINT (*Uprooting sign and planting flag in its place*): I claim this land for King Beast.

VIPER (*Advancing on* BELINDA): And I claim this gal for King Beast. Come along nice and quiet, little lady. (*He advances menacingly toward* BELINDA, *who holds up book like a talisman.*)

BELINDA (*Boldly*): Stop! (*Outlaws stop, bewildered.*) Stop in the name of Homer, Plato and Aristotle!

VIPER (*Baffled*): Who's that?

VARMINT: Must be three dudes she's got hidden around here to ambush us.

BELINDA (*Advancing to* VIPER *and yanking the picnic basket from his arm*): I will take back our picnic basket, in the name of Ovid, Seneca and Julius Caesar!

VIPER (*Frightened*): Make that *six* dudes, Varmint!

VARMINT (*Nervously*): Let's get out of here, Viper. Make tracks! (*They run off left.* BELINDA *laughs.*)

BURRITO: Ay yi yi, you were brave, Miss Belinda.

SASSAFRAS (*Awed*): Bravest thing I ever saw. Weren't you scared?

BELINDA: Librarians are never scared, Sassafras. (*She laughs.*) Perhaps I should have let them have the picnic basket. What do you think is in it?

BURRITO: Delicious chickens?

BELINDA: No, delicious *Dickens.* (*Taking books from basket, showing them to children*) See? The only food a librarian ever has on a picnic — food for thought. Books! (*All laugh.*) Now, time to go home. Back to the Bar-Be-Que Ranch. Father will be arriving home from St. Louis today. Come along. (*They exit right. "She'll Be Coming 'Round the Mountain" is played fast tempo as curtains open.*)

* * *

TIME: *A few minutes later.*

SETTING: *The rustic parlor of the Bar-Be-Que Ranch. Up*

right is door leading outside. Up left and right of center are windows draped in chintz. Center is fireplace and mantel, with portrait of a Texas Longhorn on wall above it, and a bust of Homer and two hurricane lamps on mantelpiece. Down left are desk and chair, and bookcase crammed with books. Down right and left are exits to other rooms.

AT RISE: BELINDA *stands down center, telegram in hand.* ABIGAIL *and* SASSAFRAS, *wearing aprons, stand as if in tableau:* ABIGAIL *holds broom;* SASSAFRAS *kneels with dust pan.* BURRITO *holds wicker trash basket.* HU HEE, *feather duster in hand, stands left, duster upraised.*

BELINDA: Why, this telegram is from Father. Listen. (*Reads*) "Big news, honey. Stop. You're gonna have a stepmother and stepsisters. Stop. Father and fiancée arriving on four o'clock stage. Stop." (*Looking up*) Dear Father! I'm so happy for him. (*Silence*) Aren't you all happy, too?

HU HEE (*Shaking head*): Remains to be seen, Missy Belinda. Must see honorable wife-to-be first. (*All murmur in agreement.*)

BELINDA: Why, Hu Hee, you know I trust Father's judgment. Anyone he'd choose to be Mrs. Buckthorne is certain to be perfectly lovely. Just think, new sisters, too! (*She sings slowly to tune of "She'll Be Coming 'Round the Mountain."*)

    A sublimely happy family, we will be.

OTHERS (*Singing; doubtfully*):
    We will see.

BELINDA (*Singing*):
    With a mother to confide in, just for me.

OTHERS (*Singing*):
    We will see.

BELINDA (*Singing*):
> With two sisters for a bonus —
> What a miracle's been shown us!
> We will live together, oh, so lovingly.

OTHERS (*Singing*):
> We will *see.*

BELINDA (*Speaking*): Do cheer up, all of you. This is good news. Wonderful times are ahead for all of us. (*Music to same song begins to play in background.*)

SASSAFRAS: We sure could use some good news around here. (*Does some jig steps as music tempo increases.* SASSAFRAS *starts to sing to same tune as before.*)
> Good news makes me feel like dancin' —

OTHERS (*Jigging in place; singing*):
> So do we! So do we!

SASSAFRAS (*Singing and grabbing* BURRITO *to dance, center*):
> Strut your stuff with fancy prancin',
> One-two-three —

OTHERS (*Singing*):
> One-two-three.

SASSAFRAS (*Singing*):
> With the happiness we're feelin'
> We'll go rockin' and a-reelin'
> Lift the top right off the ceilin' —
> Glo-ry be!

OTHERS (*Singing*):
> Glo-ry be!

(*All form line, dance jig steps center. At conclusion of dance, music still plays in background.* HU HEE *steps forward, speaking reflectively.*)

HU HEE: New lady-wife and daughters come from faraway St. Louis. Maybe they be like frightened little flowers.

Perhaps pine for home. We make them welcome here.
We help new lady-wife. (HU HEE *sings to same tune as
before.*)
    We must aid her and abet her —
OTHERS (*Singing*):
    Yes, siree!
SASSAFRAS (*Singing*):
    There ain't nothin' I won't get her —
OTHERS (*Singing*):
    Yes, siree.
BELINDA (*Singing*):
    We'll be happy that we met her,
OTHERS (*Singing*):
    Mark this day with a big red letter,
BURRITO (*Singing*):
    And mañana will be better,
OTHERS (*Singing*):
    We'll soon see. Yes, siree.
    (*Music continues, dance tempo, as all swing into a reel,
BELINDA do-si-do-ing down the line. Loud knocking on
door is heard. Door bursts open and MRS. POMPOSIA
SMYTHE-SMITHERS sweeps in haughtily, followed by
FASTIDIA and GAUDIA. Music stops mid-beat. Others see
them and gasp.*)
POMPOSIA: Pray tell us, where is the Buckthorne mansion? I
    am Pomposia Smythe-Smithers the Third, and these are
    my daughters, Fastidia and Gaudia.
BELINDA: Why, this is the Buckthorne ranch.
FASTIDIA: This hovel?
GAUDIA: What a dump!
POMPOSIA: Is *this* Mr. Buckthorne's domicile? (*Snootily*)
    How — quaint. (*She and daughters simultaneously hold
up lorgnettes, staring at BELINDA.*) You must be Belinda
Buckthorne.

BELINDA (*Cordially*): And you must be my stepmother-to-be. (*Crosses to embrace* POMPOSIA, *who draws away with distaste, and extends a limp hand in royal fashion. As if on signal, daughters extend their hands.*) We certainly do welcome you with open arms. (*To others*) Don't we?

ALL (*Looking at each other with foreboding*): We certainly do.

BELINDA (Eagerly): Is Father with you?

POMPOSIA (*Vaguely*): No. Your papa took a short cut across a stretch of desert called No-Man's Land, I believe.

ALL (*Together*): No-Man's Land!

BURRITO: Ay-yi-yi, the Beast just claimed that land!

FASTIDIA (*Alarmed*): Beast?

GAUDIA: What Beast?

POMPOSIA: Mr. Buckthorne never mentioned any Beast.

BELINDA (*Hastily*): It's nothing to worry about, truly, Stepmother.

POMPOSIA (*Haughtily*): Call me *Mrs. Smythe-Smithers,* Belinda, dear. (*Indicating* SASSAFRAS, BURRITO, *and* HU HEE) Are these your hired help? Have them bring in our luggage immediately.

SASSAFRAS (*Offended*): Hired help!

BELINDA: Mrs. Smythe-Smithers, these good folk are my helpers, but they are also my friends.

POMPOSIA: How gauche!

SASSAFRAS (*Arms on hips; saucily*): Miss Belinda, do we have to tote their luggage? (HU HEE *and* BURRITO *ad lib protests.*)

BELINDA: Please. Do it for me. (SASSAFRAS, HU HEE *and* BURRITO *exit, grumbling, down right.* POMPOSIA *moves about the room imperiously, looking at the furnishings through her lorgnette.* FASTIDIA *and* GAUDIA *follow her around, doing same.* BELINDA *stands apart, down left, arms folded. "Tavern in the Town" plays through action and under narration.*)

POMPOSIA: We have our work cut out for us, girls. We must turn this hovel into an abode fit for women of our station in life.

BELINDA: A hovel? Why, I decorated this house myself!

FASTIDIA: With your eyes shut, no doubt.

POMPOSIA: Take out your notebooks, girls. Make lists. (FASTIDIA *and* GAUDIA *take notebooks and small pencils from purses, following* POMPOSIA *as she whips out tape measure from purse and measures curtains, benches, door and floor.* BELINDA *stands upstage, watching unhappily.* POMPOSIA *sings to tune of "Tavern in the Town."*)

    Those dreadful drapes, they must come down,

DAUGHTERS (*Singing*):

    Must come down.

POMPOSIA (*Singing*):

    We'll have portieres sent in from town,

DAUGHTERS (*Singing*):

    In from town,

POMPOSIA (*Singing*):

    And a suite complete of Dun-can Phyfe —

BELINDA (*Singing; stamping foot*):

    You won't. You won't. Not on your life!

POMPOSIA (*Gazing upward; singing second verse*):

    I'll want a crystal chandelier —

BELINDA (*Singing*):

    Not in here!

POMPOSIA (*Singing; crossing to sideboard*):

    Some silver made by Paul Revere —

BELINDA (*Singing*):

    Much too dear!

POMPOSIA (*Singing*):
> And some servants from the British Isles,
> All curtsies, bows and cheerful smiles.
> (*She crosses to bookshelf, running finger over books, looking distastefully at fingertip; singing third verse*)
> This shabby bookshelf cannot stay.

BELINDA (*Running to bookshelf, arms outstretched protectively*):
> Yes, I say!

POMPOSIA (*Singing*):
> Put in a charming window bay —

GIRLS (*Singing*):
> Window bay —

POMPOSIA (*Strolling downstage; singing*):
> There'll be Persian rugs upon the floors,
> And carved pearl handles on the doors!

BELINDA (*Crossing center; speaking*): I don't believe this is happening. It's a nightmare. Oh, Father, Father. What have you done to us? (*Sound of hoofbeats, shots and whoops is heard from offstage. Door bursts open, and* BUCK BUCKTHORNE *runs in with* VARMINT, *who is holding a pistol to his head.* VIPER *follows with rifle. He forces women down left.*) Father!

POMPOSIA: Why, Mr. Buckthorne! What happened?

BUCK: The Beast's men caught me going across No-Man's Land. (*To* VARMINT) Go on, shoot me. I'd rather be dead than tell these women what the Beast suggested.

VARMINT: I'd just as soon shoot you, Buckthorne, but King Beast wants his proposition delivered to these women.

POMPOSIA: What proposition? We'll do anything if you'll spare dear Mr. Buckthorne.

FASTIDIA *and* GAUDIA (*Together*): *Anything.*

VIPER: King Beast wants one of you women to marry up with him. He wants a Queen Beast.

POMPOSIA, FASTIDIA *and* GAUDIA (*Gasping; ad lib*): Anything but that! Oh, no, how dreadful! (*Etc.*)

VARMINT (*Pushing pistol against* BUCKTHORNE*'s head*): Got any last words, Buckthorne?

BELINDA (*Stepping forward*): Stop — wait. *I* will go with you.

BUCK: No, Belinda. I won't let you do it.

POMPOSIA: Yes, yes, Belinda. How *sweet.* How *commendable.* Go to save your father.

BELINDA (*To* VARMINT *and* VIPER): Take me to your Beast! (VARMINT *and* VIPER *cheer as* BELINDA *marches offstage up right.* VIPER *and* VARMINT *exit.* BUCK *runs to door, protesting.*)

BUCK: I'll get you back, Belinda, if it takes every cent I have!

POMPOSIA (*Aside to* FASTIDIA *and* GAUDIA; *smirking*): With Belinda out of the way, Mr. Buckthorne is all *mine.*

FASTIDIA: All *ours,* Mama.

GAUDIA: All *ours.* (*Curtain*)

* * * * *

SCENE 2

TIME: *Later that day.*

SETTING: *The Beast's cave. There is a black backdrop painted with stalactites and stalagmites. Center stage is a rock throne: on the seat are a crown, bearskin robe, and club. Right and left of throne are trunks and boxes of loot. Down right is a campfire.*

AT RISE: *Some of the* BEAST'S BADMEN *are seated around the fire, toasting chunks of meat on long sticks. More* BADMEN *are seated around table, center, playing cards.*

Sound of roar from B.J. BEAST *is heard offstage, and* BADMEN *spring to attention.*

1ST BADMAN: Attention. King Beast is comin'!

BADMEN (*Together*): Make way for King Beast. (*Another roar is heard from off, and* B.J. BEAST *enters down left and swaggers upstage to throne. He is ill-kempt and crude, but appealing.*)

BEAST: Hail me.

BADMEN (*Together*): Hail, King Beast.

BEAST: Crown me.

1ST BADMAN (*Putting crown on* BEAST'S *head*): Yes, sir, King Beast.

BEAST: Robe me. (2ND BADMAN *puts robe around* BEAST'*s shoulders.*)

2ND BADMAN: Yes, sir, King Beast.

BEAST: Gimme my club.

3RD BADMAN: Right away, King Beast. (*Hands* BEAST *the club*)

BEAST: Now sing me the Beastly Anthem.

BADMEN (*Singing to tune of "Tramp! Tramp! Tramp!"*):
Tramp! Tramp! Tramp! King Beast is coming.
Don't make trouble or he'll shoot!
Just bow low and call him "King," (*All bow.*)

BEAST (*Singing*):
All I want is *everything* —

BADMEN (*Singing*):
So give up, give in, and give him all your loot!
(BADMEN *begin marching in place, while singing.*)
Tramp! Tramp! Tramp! King Beast is coming,
Give up, there's no use to fight.
All your worldly goods forsake,

BEAST (*Singing*):
What I want is what I take,

BADMEN (*Singing*):

For the motto of King Beast is: Might makes right!

BEAST (*Speaking*): Right! (VARMINT *enters, followed reluctantly by* BELINDA, *with* VIPER *prodding her with rifle.*)

VARMINT *and* VIPER (*Together*): Hail, King Beast.

BEAST: Did you bring me some loot?

VARMINT: Better'n that, King Beast. I brought you a *gal*. (BADMEN *whoop and whistle.*)

BEAST (*Roaring*): Quiet! Don't you know how to behave in front of a lady? Vamoose, the lot of you. We're going to have a private parley. (BADMEN *exit down left.* VARMINT *and* VIPER *remain.* VIPER *nudges* BELINDA *up center with rifle.* BELINDA *folds arms defiantly.*)

VIPER: This is Buckthorne's daughter, Belinda.

VARMINT: She'll make a good queen for you.

BEAST (*Circling* BELINDA, *ogling her, then whistling approvingly*): Well, hello, Belinda. How'd you like to be Queen of the West, gal? (BELINDA *is silent; to* VARMINT) Can't she talk?

VARMINT: She can talk, all right. She could put a parrot out of business.

BEAST: Good. Then let's get the marryin' over with. Where's the parson? (VARMINT *and* VIPER *look at each other nervously.*)

VARMINT: Viper, you were supposed to hog-tie a parson and bring him here.

VIPER: Oh, no. *You* were supposed to get the parson.

BEAST: Get me a parson. Now!

VIPER *and* VARMINT (*Together*): Yessir, King Beast. (*They run off right.*)

BEAST (*To* BELINDA; *indicating throne*): Sit yourself down, Belinda. Make yourself to home.

BELINDA: No, thank you. I have a home. This is not it.

BEAST (*Taken aback*): Huh! Feisty little gal, aren't you, Belinda?

BELINDA (*Frostily*): You may call me *Miss* Buckthorne.

BEAST: *Miss* Buckthorne, eh? Well, you can call (*Thumb to chest*) me — King.

BELINDA: Never.

BEAST (*Angrily*): What makes you so contrary? Here I am being nicer to you than I am to anybody except my ma, and you're as cold as ice. Now, why won't you call me King? I can *make* you call me King. (*He thumps chest and yells like Tarzan.* BELINDA *yawns.*) How come you didn't faint? Women always faint when I roar.

BELINDA (*Matter-of-factly*): I am a librarian. Librarians do not faint.

BEAST (*Fetching necklace from jewel box and dangling it in front of* BELINDA; *craftily*): Come on, gal. I'll give you this if you'll call me King.

BELINDA: No.

BEAST (*Crossing to trunk and holding up gown; wheedling*): How 'bout this pretty purple dress? I stole it myself.

BELINDA: No.

BEAST (*Exasperated*): Then what'll it take to make you call me King?

BELINDA (*Singing to tune of "The Flowers That Bloom in the Spring"*):
For you to be monarch of all, O Beast,
A remedial program you need.
With a knowledge of right and of wrong, at least,
An awareness of matters of state, increased,
And these words for your wisdom please heed:
You must certainly learn to *read*.

BEAST (*Singing; turning away, disgruntled*):

Well, I ain't gonna listen,
By Ginger! By Sam!
'Cause I like the kind of a King
That I am.

BELINDA (*Singing; stamping foot*):
I find you appalling!
Your manners are galling,
You're beastly and vulgar and sly.

BEAST (*Singing; facing her; hotly*):
Well, don't rearrange me,
You never will change me,
I'll always be me. Don't try!

BELINDA (*Singing second verse; wagging finger at him*):
For you to be head of society,
Your manners must be more refined.
You *must* change your shirts and bathe frequently,
You must use fine china when you're at tea,
And a napkin whenever you dine,
And be reverent, courageous and kind.

BEAST (*Singing; fingers in ears*):
Well, I ain't gonna listen,
By Ginger! By Sam!
'Cause I like the kind of a King
That I am.

BELINDA (*Singing; stamping foot again*):
I find you appalling!
I'll never stop calling —
You Beast, 'til the day that I die —

BEAST (*Singing*):
Well, don't rearrange me,
You never will change me.
I'll always be me. Don't try!

BELINDA (*Speaking*): You are impossible!

BEAST: You aren't any too *possible* yourself.

BELINDA: There are certain things I will require if you are going to keep me prisoner here.

BEAST: For instance?

BELINDA: Books. I must occupy my mind, and I intend to start a library right here.

BEAST: A library? Listen, gal. I got along my whole life without readin' and I'm not startin' now.

BELINDA (*With determination*): That remains to be seen. (*Curtain. Reprise of "The Flowers That Bloom in the Spring" and western songs may be played while scenery is changed.*)

* * * * *

SCENE 3

TIME: *Some months later.*

SETTING: *Same as Scene 2. Cave has been spruced up. The loot is stacked neatly at right. The campfire is gone. Bookshelf, table and chair are down left. BEAST's crown, robe, and club are on throne.*

AT RISE: BADMEN, *in clean plaid shirts, hair combed, books open in their hands, are seated center on cushions in a row across stage. BELINDA sits at table.*

BELINDA (*To BADMEN*): You gentlemen have made phenomenal progress these past months.

BADMEN (*Together*): Thank you, Miss Buckthorne.

BELINDA: Now, let us all read together from the Declaration of Independence. (*Sound of BEAST roaring is heard from offstage. BADMEN pay no attention.*)

BADMEN (*Reading; together*): "We hold these truths to be self-evident: that all men are created equal . . ." (*BEAST enters grandly, still ill-kempt, thumping his chest, giving Tarzan yell.*)

BEAST: Hail me!

BADMEN (*Continuing to read*): "That they are endowed by their creator with certain unalienable rights . . ."

BEAST (*Louder*): Crown me! Robe me! Give me my club, consarn you!

BADMEN (*Still reading*): "That among these are life, liberty and the pursuit of happiness."

BEAST (*Roaring*): Quiet! This is *King Beast talkin'!*

1ST BADMAN (*Turning to* BEAST): Simmer down, B.J. Accordin' to this book we are not your subjects anymore.

2ND BADMAN: We're your equals. See? (*Pointing to book*) Right here on page twenty-five.

BADMEN (*Together*): We're *equals.*

BEAST (*Sarcastically*): Equals? I'm more equal than any six of you! Now, get out and grab me some land.

2ND BADMAN: We don't *grab* land anymore.

3RD BADMAN: We buy it and pay for it, fair and square.

BADMEN (*Together*): Fair and square.

BEAST: That's against all my principles! (*To* BADMEN) You smell like soft soap and shavin' lotion. Get out!

4TH BADMAN (*To* BELINDA): May we be excused, Miss Buckthorne?

BELINDA: You may. (BADMEN *put books in neat pile on table.*)

BADMEN (*Together*): Afternoon, Miss Buckthorne. So long, B.J. (*They bow to* BELINDA *and exit down right, except for* 1ST BADMAN.)

1ST BADMAN (*To* BEAST): We're going to pursue us some happiness.

BEAST (*Furious*): Get out and stay out! (1ST BADMAN *rushes out.* BEAST *throws book after him, crosses down left to apron and stands with arms folded.* BELINDA *crosses down right on apron.* BEAST *speaks aside.*) She's no bigger'n a roadrunner, weighs less than a hundred pounds soakin' wet, and she's *ruinin'* me. And what's worse — she's gettin' to me. Yesterday I almost opened a book. Tomorrow I might take a bath.

BELINDA (*Aside*): Though I have won over his men, he remains aloof and apart. A Beast to the end. How can I win him over?

BEAST (*Aside*): I could tie her up and gag her. I could shut her in a dark room. But then she'd hate me. She's none too fond of me now, but I couldn't live if she hated me.

BELINDA (*Aside*): He has such power. Such potential. What a king he'd be! I could grow almost—fond—of him. (*The final measures of "The Flowers That Bloom in the Spring" are heard, and* BELINDA *starts to sing.*)

If I could but reach him —

The things I could teach him!

How proud and how princely he'd be.

BEAST (*Singing*):

I'd talk to her often,

If only she'd soften —

I might even drink her *tea*!

(BEAST *crosses slowly to* BELINDA, *who turns to meet him. He addresses her shyly.*) Belinda — I mean, Miss Buckthorne.

BELINDA: Why, that's the first time you have addressed me as "Miss Buckthorne," Beast — that is — B.J.

BEAST: I won't beat around any bushes. I want to know straight out. Can you love a Beast? Because that's what I am and that's what I'll always be.

BELINDA (*Hesitating, then sadly*): No, B.J. I cannot love you as a Beast. That is how I will always feel. (BEAST *turns away, crushed. Sound of whoops from* VARMINT *and* VIPER *are heard from off.*)

BEAST (*Starting off left*): That's Varmint and Viper. Some-thin's up. (*He pauses, turns, bows awkwardly to* BEL-INDA.) Excuse me, Miss Buckthorne?

BELINDA (*Touched*): Of course, B.J. (BEAST *exits right.* CHICKEN FEATHER *crawls in cautiously, down left, looks around, sniffs air, wets finger, holds it up, then hoots softly three times.*) Chicken Feather! (*He motions her to silence.* SASSAFRAS *enters, finger to lips.*) Sassafras! (BELINDA *motions them down right.*) I can't tell you how glad I am to see you! (BEAST, VARMINT *and* VIPER *enter, unseen by others.*) How is Father?

SASSAFRAS: He's got trouble, Miss Belinda.

CHICKEN FEATHER: Ugh. Bad trouble.

SASSAFRAS: That widder woman, Pomposia Smythe-Smithers, is a *confidence* woman. A crook!

BEAST (*Aside*): Pomposia Smythe-Smithers! Aha!

BELINDA: What do you mean, Sassafras?

SASSAFRAS: She and her daughters travel around the country marryin' up with fellers. Then when she's got their money, she runs off, changes her name, and leaves 'em with empty pockets and empty hearts.

BELINDA: She mustn't marry my father!

CHICKEN FEATHER: Ugh, too late! Wedding tonight!

BELINDA: What? Chicken Feather, lead me out of this cave. Hurry! *I must stop that wedding.* (CHICKEN FEATHER *runs off right, followed by* BELINDA *and* SASSAFRAS. VARMINT *and* VIPER *run center.* BEAST *follows them, slowly, rubbing chin.*)

VARMINT (*Pointing off*): She's running out on you, boss!

VIPER: Want us to stop her? (BEAST *is silent.*) Boss?

BEAST (*To himself*): So, Pomposia Smythe-Smithers, our paths cross again. The only thing you understand is force, and you'll get it. (*To* VARMINT *and* VIPER) Fetch me my gun belt and my silver-studded six-guns.

VARMINT (*Eagerly*): Are you ridin' with us, boss? (BEAST *nods.*)

VIPER: Hot diggity dog! We're going to go grabbin' and robbin' again!

BEAST (*Aside*): Belinda will hate me for what I'm going to do. Still I have to be a beast, so I can rescue her pa. (*Takes small book from table and slips it inside vest, above heart*) I'll take one of her books to bring me luck. (*Thumping chest and roaring*) King Beast rides again! (VARMINT *and* VIPER *shout approval, shooting pistols into air. Quick curtain. Optional music and dance interlude:* COWBOYS *and* GALS *may perform songs and dances in front of curtain while scenery is changed.*)

* * * * *

SCENE 4

TIME: *That night.*

SETTING: *Same as Scene 1, but parlor is redecorated, with drapes at windows, and candelabra and bouquets on mantel. Ornate picture of a castle hangs over fireplace. Paper fan is in fireplace. On the sideboard are punch bowl and cups. Folding chairs have been set up, facing fireplace, with aisle center and red runner up and down stage.*

AT RISE: BELINDA *tiptoes on, surveys decor.*

BELINDA (*Aghast*): What deplorable taste! Why, these new furnishings must have cost Father a fortune!

POMPOSIA (*Offstage*): Come along, girls. We must see if Parson Worthy has arrived. (BELINDA *runs upstage and hides behind drapes, left, as* POMPOSIA, FASTIDIA *and* GAUDIA, *all in bridal attire, enter left. They carry long scarves.* POMPOSIA *carries a bank book and a bouquet with a small revolver concealed in the flowers.*) The parson's not here yet. Just as well. We must run through our plans. (*She nods significantly at* GAUDIA *and* FASTIDIA, *who nod back.*)

GAUDIA: Are we doing the bank caper this time? Clean him out after the ceremony?

POMPOSIA: Exactly. (*Waving bank book*) As soon as the Parson pronounces us man and wife, Buckthorne's entire fortune will be mine.

FASTIDIA: *Ours,* Mama. We have the horses waiting out back.

GAUDIA: I unlatched the kitchen door.

POMPOSIA: Very good. After the wedding we'll meet in the kitchen —

FASTIDIA: Slip out the back door —

GAUDIA: Ride like sixty to the bank, and clean out the Buckthorne account.

POMPOSIA: And then — we'll go to California, to find a rich miner with a lonesome look.

ALL (*Together*): California, here we come! (*As they laugh,* BELINDA *marches out from behind curtain.*)

BELINDA: On the contrary! You are going nowhere — except to *jail.*

FASTIDIA *and* GAUDIA (*Ad lib*): Belinda! What are you doing here? (*Etc.* POMPOSIA *crosses upstage.*)

POMPOSIA (*Purring*): There, there, Belinda! We were only joking. Weren't we, girls? (*Aside, to* FASTIDIA *and* GAUDIA) Quick! The old scarf trick — bind her and put her behind the drapes. Hurry, I hear someone coming! (FASTIDIA *and* GAUDIA *catch* BELINDA *by surprise.* FASTIDIA *gags her,* GAUDIA *binds her hands, as* POMPOSIA *ties her feet. They push her behind the drapes, left, as* BUCK *enters with* PARSON WORTHY, *who carries small black book.*)

BUCK: Pomposia, darlin', looky here. Parson Worthy's come, so the weddin' can commence to begin.

POMPOSIA: How wonderful! (PARSON *stands up center.* POMPOSIA *and daughters stand left,* BUCK, *right.* ABIGAIL, SASSAFRAS, BURRITO, HU HEE, CHICKEN FEATHER, TROOPER HOOPER *and* CAPTAIN MCREADY *enter left and right and sit on folding chairs.* JIMMY TONSILS *enters and stands right, a little apart, strumming "Wedding March" on guitar.*)

BUCK: If only Belinda were here!

FASTIDIA: She would have been here —

GAUDIA: But she's all tied up.

SASSAFRAS: She's here somewhere (POMPOSIA *looks at her sharply.*) in spirit.

PARSON: Dearly beloved, we are gathered here to join these folks in holy wedlock. Afore I begin, is there anyone here who knows any reason why these two lovebirds may not be joined in marriage? (*Sound of* BELINDA *moaning is heard from drapes, which move as she struggles.*)

BURRITO (*Pointing to drapes*): Ay yi yi! A ghost!

POMPOSIA (*As* FASTIDIA *and* GAUDIA *nudge drapes into place*): Continue, Parson.

FASTIDIA: It's only the wind. (*Sound of hoofbeats is heard from offstage.* POMPOSIA *nudges* PARSON.)

POMPOSIA: Hurry up.

PARSON (*Thumbing through book*): Where was I? (*Sound of hoofbeats gets louder*) Oh, yes. Do you, Pomposia Smythe-Smithers the Third . . .

POMPOSIA (*Interrupting*): I do. So does he. Quickly, pronounce us wed.

PARSON: Hold your horses. Let me find the place. (*Ex-*

amines book) Here it is. I now pronounce you — (*Shots and whoops are heard from offstage.* BEAST *bursts on up right, shooting into air, followed by* VARMINT *and* VIPER.)

BEAST: Stop the weddin'!

POMPOSIA: Bartholomew! Bartholomew Jasper Beast!

BEAST: Pomposia Smythe-Smithers the Third, alias Gilda the Gold-Digger. You had me under your spell once. You made me the Beast I am today. Well, the weddin' is off. You've bilked your last bozo, Gilda. (*Others gasp.*)

BUCK: What's going on here, Pomposia? (POMPOSIA *pulls revolver from bouquet as she moves toward drapes, where* BELINDA *is hidden.*)

POMPOSIA: Don't move, or I'll shoot. Yes, I am Gilda the Gold-Digger. As long as there's a sucker in this world, I intend to go on gold-digging. (*To* FASTIDIA *and* GAUDIA) Get Belinda and bring her with us.

BUCK (*As* FASTIDIA *and* GAUDIA *pull* BELINDA *from behind drapes*): Belinda! My little Belinda, tied up like a steer going to market! Somebody — save her!

BEAST (*Running upstage*): I'll save her, Buckthorne. (*Placing himself between* BELINDA *and* POMPOSIA) Get away from my gal! (POMPOSIA *shoots* BEAST *and he crumples to floor.* BELINDA *moans through her gag.* HOOPER *drags* BEAST *down center, as* CHICKEN FEATHER *and* MCREADY *grab* POMPOSIA, FASTIDIA, *and* GAUDIA. BUCK *unties* BELINDA.)

MCREADY (*To* POMPOSIA): Gilda the Gold-Digger, you and your low-down accomplices are under arrest. (*Hands gun to* CHICKEN FEATHER) March 'em over to the jail, Chicken Feather. (CHICKEN FEATHER *marches* POMPOSIA, FASTIDIA *and* GAUDIA *off left.* BELINDA *rushes to* BEAST, *kneels and puts his head on her lap.* VARMINT *and* VIPER *kneel beside her.* MCREADY *takes* BEAST*'s pulse as* HOOPER *fans him with hat.* BELINDA *sobs,* MCREADY *consoles her.*) There, there, little lady, his pulse is still goin' strong. He's not dead yet. (*Music to "The Flowers that Bloom in the Spring" plays softly.*)

BELINDA: Courage, dear Beast. Courage!

VARMINT: Aw, shucks, Boss. Don't go and die on us.

VIPER: We need you, Boss. Who's gonna snatch ranches and grab land when you're gone?

BEAST (*Raising on elbow*): No more snatching and grabbing. Promise me you'll give back every inch of land I've taken, and all that loot.

VARMINT: But, Boss —

BEAST: Promise!

VIPER *and* VARMINT (*Together*): We promise.

BEAST (*To* BELINDA): Can you forgive me, Belinda? I didn't want to be a beast anymore, but I had to be, just this one more time, to save you and your pa from a fate worse than death: Bankruptcy. (*He falls back on* BELINDA*'s lap.*)

BELINDA: My poor, dear Beast! There is nothing to forgive. Why, you have proved yourself noble and generous and brave. In fact, with a clear conscience, I can now call you — King!

BEAST (*Grinning, raising head*): Did you hear that, folks? At last — she called me King. I can die happy! (*He goes limp. All gasp and press closer around* BEAST.)

HOOPER: Has he breathed his last, Captain?

MCREADY: I don't know. He was shot in the chest, but there's not a drop of blood; something stopped that bullet cold. (*Pulling book with hole in it from* BEAST*'s vest*)

It's a book! Why, this is a miracle. (*All applaud and cheer, as* BEAST *staggers to his feet, assisted by* BELINDA, *who holds book for all to see.*)

BELINDA: A miracle indeed. It's Shakespeare's play — "All's Well That Ends Well"! (*All cheer.*)

PARSON (*Starting off right*): If you've no further need of a Parson, I'll be going.

HU HEE: Please to wait, reverent gentleman. (*Crossing down center, joining hands of* ABIGAIL *and* HOOPER, BELINDA *and* BEAST) Ancient sage say: "Never put off marrying until tomorrow when you can marry today."

ABIGAIL: Truer words were never spoken. Why waste a perfectly good parson? (*To* HOOPER) Henry, pop the question.

HOOPER (*On one knee*): Miss Abigail, will you —

ABIGAIL (*Interrupting*): You know I will, Henry.

BEAST (*Hand on heart*): Miss Buckthorne, will you do me the honor of marryin' up with me?

BELINDA: B.J., will you learn to read?

BEAST: I'll swallow an entire encyclopedia and a dictionary if it'll please you. (*Smooths hair*)

BELINDA (*Joyfully*): Then I will consent to be your true and faithful partner with the greatest pleasure.

BEAST: Was that a "yes"?

BUCK: Take it or leave it, son. That's the closest to a yes you'll get from Belinda Buckthorne.

BEAST: I'll take it! (*All cheer.* PARSON *and two couples cross up center, forming tableau, with* MCREADY *standing next to* ABIGAIL *and* HOOPER, BUCK *next to* BELINDA *and* BEAST. *Others turn to audience, and sing.*)

ALL (*Singing to tune of "She'll Be Coming 'Round the Mountain"*):

Everything is fine and dandy,
Got no doubt.
Spread the word there's smiles
And sunshine, hereabout.
Every wrong has been all-righted,
And our lovers are united,
Naturally we're plumb dee-lighted,
Shout it out! Shout it out!

JIMMY TONSILS (*Singing*):

Swing your partner,
Promenade her when I call —
Do si do, away you go,
Around the hall,
Raise the roof and raise the rafter,
Raise some cane with joy and laughter,
We'll live happy — ever after,
After all!

(*Music continues, faster, as all dance. At conclusion of dance, curtains close.*)

THE END

Belinda and the Beast

Production Notes

Characters: 19 male; 10 female (parts may be doubled to reduce cast size).

Playing Time: 35 minutes.

Costumes: Traditional cowboy outfit and guitar for Jimmy Tonsils; coolie costume and queue for Hu Hee; Indian costume for Chicken Feather. Captain McReady and Trooper Hooper wear Cavalry uniforms. Abigail wears simple print dress, has flowers in hair. Belinda has plain dress, may wear hair in bun; Burrito and Sassafras wear tattered clothes, may be barefoot. B.J. Beast has scraggly hair, beard, and a generally unkempt, crude appearance, and Varmint, Viper and Four Badmen are similar in appearance. In Scene 3, Badmen change to clean plaid shirts and jeans, and hair is combed. Pomposia, Fastidia and Gaudia wear ostentatious dresses, wear lorgnettes and carry purses containing small notebooks and pencils. They change to wedding finery, carry long scarves, in Scene 4. Buck is a well-dressed rancher, with string tie and gold belt buckle; Parson Worthy wears black suit, white collar. Cowboys and Gals wear traditional western outfits.

Properties: Guitar; small gong and striker; bouquets of flowers (Pomposia has one with toy revolver concealed in it); books; flag with skull and crossbones; prop rifle; picnic basket containing books; telegram; dustpan; broom; wicker trash basket; feather duster; tape measure; long sticks with chunks of meat on them; playing cards; necklace; purple dress; bank book; small preacher's Bible.

Setting: Scene 1, Before Rise: At center is pole with sign, reading NO MAN'S LAND. NO WOMAN'S NEITHER. BEWARE OF BEAST. There is a large rock at right, and at left, a water tower. At Rise: Parlor of the Bar-Be-Que Ranch. Door leading outside is up right. Up left and right of center are windows draped in chintz. Fireplace and mantel are center, and portrait of Texas Longhorn is on wall above it, with bust of Homer and two hurricane lamps on mantelpiece. Desk and chair, and bookcase crammed with books, are down left. Down right and left are exits to other rooms. Scene 2: Beast's cave. Black backdrop has stalactites and stalagmites painted on it. Rock throne is center—crown, bearskin robe, and club are on throne. Trunks and boxes of loot are right and left of throne. Campfire is down right. Scene 3: Same as Scene 2, but loot is stacked neatly at right, campfire is gone, and bookshelf, table and chair are down left. Scene 4: Same as Scene 1, but parlor is redecorated, with new drapes at windows, and candelabra and bouquets on mantel. Pretentious picture of castle hangs over the fireplace. Paper fan is in fireplace. On sideboard are punch bowl and cups, and folding chairs are set up, facing fireplace, with aisle center and red runner up and down stage.

Lighting: No special effects.

Sound: Offstage hoofbeats, gunshots, hooting, whooping, roaring, as indicated in text. Music for songs may be provided by live musicians, who may be seated onstage, or by recorded offstage music. Jimmy Tonsils may accompany himself on guitar, or recorded guitar music may be played under his songs.

ROWDY KATE

Rowdy Kate

*A Western "adaptation" of Shakespeare's
"The Taming of the Shrew"*

Characters

MIKE MACADOO
CHUCKAWALLA
BRONC
PIGGY } *cowpokes*
CROWBAIT
GEEZER, *an old prospector*
MAYOR HOBSON
ANNABELLE
CLARABELLE
LULUBELLE } *schoolmarms*
DAISYBELLE
HORSESHOE TENNY, *a cowboy*
BLANCHE MILLIONOLA
PERCY LANCELOT LOVELACE
BIG BART MILLIONOLA
KATE MILLIONOLA
TRICKY PETE PORTER
GRUESOME MOE
SHERIFF SAM
PARSON EVEREADY

SCENE 1

BEFORE RISE: *There is an overture performed by piano, or, if possible, by a small group of musicians in the orchestra, composed of piano, guitar, banjo, accordion or harmonica. They play fast medley of songs performed in play, including "Bill Bailey," "Red River Valley," "The Streets of Laredo," and "Beautiful Dreamer."*

* * *

TIME: *Way back when . . . in the 1880's.*

SETTING: *The Greasy Gulch Saloon in New Paducah, New Mexico. Up center there is long bar, with five stools in front of it. Posters and signs hang on wall behind bar. They read:* THE NEW PADUCAH GREASY GULCH SALOON; CHECK YOUR GUNS AT THE BAR; IF YOU'RE WANTED BY THE MARSHAL, YOU'RE NOT WANTED HERE; DON'T BLEED ON THE CARPET; GO OUTSIDE TO SHOOT; THESE PREMISES INSPECTED MONTHLY BY SHERIFF SAM. *Table with chairs around it stands down left and long bench is against wall, right. There is swinging door up right, with sign hanging over it, reading* WELCOME. *Decorative bunting is tacked to walls. A pre-painted banner, turned so audience cannot read it, is draped over one end of bar.*

AT RISE: MIKE MACADOO, *bartender, stands behind bar, lazily wiping surface with cloth. Cowpokes* CHUCKA-WALLA, BRONC, PIGGY *and* CROWBAIT, *wearing their Stetsons, sit at table down left, playing poker.* GEEZER *is lying on bench, on his back, with his Stetson over his eyes. He snores loudly and whistles "Dixie" on outgoing breath. Flyswatter dangles from one hand.*

MIKE (*To cowpokes*): Listen to that. Old Geezer is sawing himself a wagonload of wood.

CHUCKAWALLA: Sure is. Geezer's the only feller I know who can snore and whistle "Dixie" at the same time. (MAYOR HOBSON, *wearing top hat, frock coat, and ribbon reading* WELCOME *across his chest, bustles in through swinging door.*)

MAYOR HOBSON: So this is where I find you cowpokes! Lollygagging around, instead of decorating the soda parlor. Cover up that disgusting saloon sign, MacAdoo. Crowbait, give him a hand. (MIKE *and* CROWBAIT *lift banner from bar and tack it over saloon signs, on wall behind bar. Banner reads,* NEW PADUCAH SODA PARLOR. *They put up additional signs reading,* LADIES MORE THAN WELCOME; NO SMOKING; NO CHEWING; NO HATS ON HEADS; THESE PREMISES INSPECTED DAILY BY SHERIFF SAM.)

CHUCKAWALLA: Morning, Mayor Hobson. Want to sit in?

MAYOR: You boys get your carcasses right up from there. There are ladies on their way to New Paducah.

BRONC: Ladies? (CHUCKAWALLA *covers poker chips with his hat.*)

MAYOR: Four schoolmarms, proper as you please, are coming in on the next stage, and it's due any minute.

MIKE: Who invited them?

MAYOR: *I* invited them. This town needs respectable folk. New Paducah has got to settle down and grow up. Why, we're on our way to being bypassed by civilization. We're on our way to being a ghost town, and I don't intend to be Mayor of any ghost town. You fellows don't know it, but the West is changing right under your sunburnt noses. (MAYOR *sings to tune of "Red River Valley."*)

> There are wagons of settlers a-coming.
> Maws and Paws, and their families, too;
> They are searching for towns calm and peaceful,
> Full of churches and schools bright and new.

MIKE (*Singing*):
>   Yes, the day of the outlaw is over . . .

CHUCKAWALLA (*Singing*):
>   You can't shoot up the town anymore . . .

BRONC (*Singing*):
>   For the kiddies are frightened of gunplay . . .

PIGGY (*Singing*):
>   And the ladies are not fond of gore.

MAYOR (*Singing*):
>   Put away all those marked cards and pistols . . .
>   (CHUCKAWALLA *scoops cards and poker chips into his hat and puts them behind bar.*)
>   Look alive, you must be at your best . . .
>   (*Smacks* GEEZER *with flyswatter.* GEEZER *sits up, protesting.*)

GEEZER (*Speaking*): I've been awake the whole time!

MAYOR (*Singing*):
>   For the homesteading folks are a-coming,
>   And a new day has dawned for the West.

ALL (*Singing*):
>   Oh, the homesteading folks are a-coming,
>   And a new day has dawned for the West.

MAYOR: Geezer, get up there by the doors and keep your eyes peeled for the stage. (GEEZER *crosses to swinging door, yawns and looks out, shading his eyes.* MAYOR *speaks like a drill sergeant.*) Line up, you cowpokes. You've got to be inspected afore you're fit to welcome ladies. (*Cowpokes shuffle over to barstools and line up.* MAYOR *inspects each one critically.*) Chuckawalla, what in tarnation is holding your shirt together?

CHUCKAWALLA: Barbed wire.

MAYOR: I swear, you are the sloppiest bunch of cowhands I

ever saw. Bronc, that vest smells peculiar. What's it made of?

BRONC: It's not peculiar. It's my best horse blanket.

MAYOR: Give it back to the horse. Piggy, looks as if you've been digging for gold with your bare knuckles. Keep your hands behind your back when the womenfolk come. (*He takes* CROWBAIT'*s battered, bullet-riddled hat, and pokes his fingers through it.*) Sufferin' dogies, Crowbait, it's a good thing your head isn't as full of holes as your hat.

GEEZER (*Turning from door, excitedly*): The stage is here! The schoolmarms are coming up the street, and they're pretty as bluebonnets in June. (*Looks out again*)

MAYOR: Attention! (*Cowpokes stand at attention.*) Now I want you to give these here ladies a real western welcome. You have to give them the idea that this is the only town in the West for them to settle in.

MIKE: Wait a minute, Mayor Hobson. We've got to be honest. We have to tell them about you-know-who.

MAYOR (*Alarmed*): Don't you dare! Don't any of you say one word about you-know-who!

GEEZER (*From door*): They're here. They're comin' right in. (MIKE *crosses to door. He and* GEEZER *hold door open as* ANNABELLE, CLARABELLE, LULUBELLE, *and* DAISYBELLE *enter.*)

MAYOR: Welcome, ladies! Welcome to New Paducah!

MAYOR, MIKE, GEEZER *and* COWPOKES (*Singing to tune of* "*Bill Bailey*"):
Welcome to New Paducah, welcome to town,
We surely hope you'll stay.
We've got a brand-new church,
A school and a bank, open for trade all day.

MAYOR (*Singing*):
Oh, you don't need heaps of money —

MIKE (*Singing*):
> Just willing hands —

GEEZER (*Singing*):
> And the grit to do your best.

MEN (*Singing*):
> We'll settle you in, with a shake and a grin, to —
> The greatest little town in the West.

GEEZER (*Singing*):
> We really mean it —
> (*Cowpokes sashay across stage, shake girls' hands and bow.*)

MEN (*Singing*):
> The greatest little town in the West!

MIKE (*Singing*):
> That's New Paducah.

MEN (*Singing*):
> The greatest little town in the West!
> (*Cowpokes go down on one knee and extend one arm forward, and one back.*)

MAYOR: Welcome, ladies. (*Motioning to bench*) Won't you please sit down? (*Reprise of "Bill Bailey" is played, as schoolmarms sit on bench right. Cowpokes sashay to bar stools and sit*). Ahem. . . . As Mayor of this up-and-coming town, I want to say how delightful it is to welcome such fair and charming creatures to New Paducah. Things are looking up. Yes, indeedy. Ladies (*Gesturing*) — these here are some of the menfolk of the town (*Aside*) — such as they be.

COWPOKES (*Together*): Howdy, ladies.

SCHOOLMARMS (*Ad lib*): How do you do? Pleased to meet you. (*Etc.*)

ANNABELLE (*Giggling*): I expect we ought to introduce ourselves. I'm Annabelle.

CLARABELLE (*Nodding*): Clarabelle.

LULUBELLE: Lulubelle.

DAISYBELLE: Daisybelle. (*She giggles.*)

GEEZER: Well, ding-dong, the bells are a-ringin' today!

ANNABELLE: We are looking forward to many happy days teaching the dear little children of your community.

CLARABELLE: How many dear little children do you have here?

MAYOR: Well — to tell the truth —

CROWBAIT: We don't have any children here.

GEEZER: We used to have a child here, but he grew up to be Crowbait! Haw, haw, haw!

LULUBELLE (*Aghast*): Are we to understand that you have invited four schoolmarms to teach in a town with no children?

MAYOR: Oh, we'll have children — a wagonload, in a month or two.

DAISYBELLE: But whom will we teach in the meantime?

PIGGY: How about teaching us, ma'am? We're mighty ignorant.

BRONC: Oh, yes, ma'am. There's nobody more ignorant than Piggy.

ANNABELLE: Oh, my. We hadn't planned on teaching great, big, grown men.

DAISYBELLE (*Coyly*): We could force ourselves.

LULUBELLE: It might be fun! I mean, it might be a real challenge (*Clears throat*) — educationally speaking, that is.

ANNABELLE: Well — before we accept your generous offer, we have a few questions to ask about the town. Now, do you have one of those shocking dance halls?

BRONC: No, ma'am.

CLARABELLE: Do you have a low, vulgar saloon?

PIGGY: No, ma'am.

LULUBELLE: Do you have any ruffians or rowdies or wild persons? (*Men look at each other sheepishly.*)

ANNABELLE: Come on, speak up. Do you have any bad men here?

CROWBAIT (*Shaking his head vigorously*): No, ma'am. No bad *men*.

GEEZER: That's right! No bad *men!*

MIKE: Sh-h-h! (MIKE *pulls* GEEZER's *hat down over his face.*)

DAISYBELLE: Oh, Annabelle, let's stay.

ANNABELLE: Well, the town seems respectable enough. All right. Mr. Mayor, on behalf of the ladies and myself, we accept. We'll stay.

MEN (*Ad lib*): Whoopee! Hooray! Three cheers for the ladies! (*Etc.*)

MAYOR: That's real nice. As I said before, things are looking up. Now you cowpokes take these ladies for a tour of the town. Show 'em the new well, and the new hotel, and the new school. Go on now. Skedaddle. (*There is a reprise of "Bill Bailey," as each cowpoke takes a schoolmarm on his arm. All exit through swinging door, held open by* GEEZER *and* MIKE. *Before they can close door,* HORSESHOE TENNY, *a cheerful, bumbling cowboy, strides in.*)

HORSESHOE: Well, howdy there. I'm a wandering stranger with mighty dry tonsils. Can I wet my whistle?

MIKE: If you want to wet your whistle here, you'll have to settle for a lemonade. (HORSESHOE *shakes his head, then shrugs and sits at table.*)

HORSESHOE: A lemonade, eh. Well, if that's all you got, bring it. (*He takes out a pack of cards.*) Anybody want to play a hand of poker?

MAYOR: Put your cards away, stranger. No poker playing

allowed. (MIKE *brings lemonade on tray.*)

GEEZER: I'll play you a hand of Old Maid, if you want.

HORSESHOE (*Scratching his head*): Dogies, this is a *weird* town. When do the dancing girls start the show?

MAYOR (*Crossing to* HORSESHOE; *menacingly*): Stranger, you'd best be just passing through. This town is not for the likes of you. We don't cater to dancing girls. There are only nice, decent schoolmarms here.

GEEZER: None of them's taken so far. You could marry one and settle down. We could use new folks here.

HORSESHOE: Me? Horseshoe Tenny, the last free man in six counties? Me — settle down? No, sir. Gals are pretty to look at, but I'm just a window-shopper. I wouldn't want a gal for keeps. No, sir. (BLANCHE MILLIONOLA, *wearing ruffles and ribbons, enters through swinging door, followed by her tutor,* PERCY LANCELOT LOVELACE. *Dramatic chord is played.* HORSESHOE TENNY *gapes at* BLANCHE. *He starts to stand up, then flops down into his chair, hand on his heart. The song, "Hearts and Flowers," is played softly behind dialogue.*) Oh, be still, my heart! (*To* MIKE) Who is shc? Who is that be-yoo-ti-ful gal?

MIKE: That's Miss Blanche Millionola, the purtiest gal in town. Her paw is Big Bart Millionola, richest man in all of the six desert counties. Hey — I thought you were just a window-shopper.

HORSESHOE: I have now become a customer in the department store of romance.

MIKE: I advise you to forget Miss Blanche.

HORSESHOE (*Making sheep's eyes*): I will never forget Miss Blanche.

BLANCHE (*Mincing over to* MAYOR): Mr. Mayor. Mr. Mayor. I couldn't wait to tell you the good news.

MAYOR: Miss Blanche, I hope you're not going to tell me what I think you're going to tell me, because if it's what you told me before, I don't want to hear it.

BLANCHE: Oh, but you must be the first to know. My dear tutor, Percival Lancelot Lovelace, and I have had a meeting of minds.

GEEZER: Oh-oh. I'd best watch the door for trouble. (*He crosses to door and stands looking out anxiously.*)

MAYOR: Oh, no!

BLANCHE: Oh, yes. Percy and I are engaged (*Turning*), aren't we, Percy darling?

PERCY: Raw-ther.

MAYOR: Miss Blanche, this is the third tutor you have been engaged to this month. Each time your engagement has been busted up violently in this very building. Please, if you want to get engaged, get engaged in some other town. (*Sounds of shots and loud whooping are heard from offstage.*)

GEEZER: Too late! Everyone take cover. (*He hides behind bench; MIKE ducks behind bar; MAYOR HOBSON runs behind bar. Offstage, schoolmarms shriek in terror. Volley of shots is heard, followed by loud, dramatic musical chord. ROWDY KATE bursts in through swinging door, shooting into air. PERCY runs for cover and cowers under table.*)

KATE (*Roaring*): Where is he? Where is that little tutor who thinks he's going to marry my sister?

BLANCHE (*Wailing*): Oh, Kate, you've spoiled things again. I'm going to tell Paw. (*She runs down right, and exits, bawling loudly.*)

KATE: Go on, tell Paw. I'm not going to be sister-in-law to a goggling bookworm with a face like a pan of sourdough. Where is he? Where's that tutor? (*She spies PERCY under table and drags him out, feet first.*) Come on and stand up like a man — if you're able! (PERCY, *cowering, stands up, his hands raised.*)

PERCY (*Shaking nervously*): Yes, Miss Kate. Whatever you say, Miss Kate.

KATE: There's a stage leaving for St. Louis right now. Get aboard and don't get off until you see the riverboats. March! (*She fires at his feet. There is more screaming from offstage.* PERCY *dances out swinging door.* CHUCKAWALLA *and* CROWBAIT *enter, carrying* ANNABELLE, *who has fainted. They put her on bench.*)

CHUCKAWALLA: Look what you've done, Kate. Miss Annabelle fainted plumb away. (MAYOR *rises cautiously.*)

MAYOR: Why'd you bother your pretty little sister again, Kate? She only wants to get married. That's not a federal offense.

KATE: Now, you listen, everybody, and you listen good. (*She shoots into air.*) I'm telling you for the last time. There'll be no weddings in New Paducah. No weddings at all — until —

ALL: Until what?

KATE: Until *my* wedding. (ANNABELLE *revives and sits up groggily.*) Well? Any of you gents want to propose? (*There is silence.*) No? Well, I wouldn't have you if you did. Remember — until Kate gets hitched, nobody gets hitched. (*She shoots twice into air, spins guns around her fingers and stalks off through swinging door.*)

ANNABELLE (*To* MAYOR): Oh! You didn't say a word about *her.* I expected rattlesnakes and cactus, but nothing like *her.* We can't stay, Mayor. (*She stands.*) I just don't see how we can stay in this town. (*She exits, nose in air, up right, through door.* BIG BART MILLIONOLA *enters down right.*)

BIG BART: Blanche told me about Kate's ruckus. I'm surely sorry for all the trouble my daughter's caused you. Whatever she did, I'll pay the damages. (*He flashes wad of bills*.)

MAYOR (*Crossing center*): Put your money away, Big Bart. Money is not the answer now.

GEEZER: No, sir!

MAYOR: This town is not safe for man nor beast with Rowdy Kate shooting things up most every week. Bart, I'm sorry, but I have to take drastic action. I hereby declare that Kate Millionola is to be treated as a common outlaw.

CHUCKAWALLA: Atta boy, Mayor!

MAYOR: I will personally see that Circulatin' Sam the Sheriff rounds her up and brings her in.

CROWBAIT: Hooray!

MAYOR: When she's brought here, I will proclaim that she is to be permanently banished from the town of New Paducah. If she ever, *ever* shows her face in this town again, she is to be tarred and feathered and ridden out on a rail.

CHUCKAWALLA *and* CROWBAIT (*Cheering*): Whoopee! (BIG BART *shakes his head, crossing downstage.*)

BIG BART: Poor little Kate. All she needs is a firm hand. Somewhere . . . somewhere there's got to be a man who can tame my Rowdy Kate! (*Curtain falls slowly, as reprise of "Hearts and Flowers" is played.*)

* * * * *

SCENE 2

SETTING: *The outskirts of New Paducah. The scene is played in front of curtain.*

BEFORE CURTAIN: TRICKY PETE PORTER *and his sidekick,* GRUESOME MOE, *enter down right.* TRICKY PETE *wears long fur coat and fur hat.* MOE *wears flowing robe and turban, pushes wheelbarrow decorated with signs, reading,* COUNT PETRUSHKA'S MYSTIC ORIENTAL OINTMENT. TRICKY PETE *stops, looks around as if lost.* MOE *takes out map.*

MOE: Map says we're a couple of miles from a hick town called New Paducah. Never heard of it.

TRICKY PETE (*Taking out pack of cards and riffling them*): New Paducah, eh? I wonder if the citizens of New Paducah are ready for a little lesson in blackjack? (*Sound of hoofbeats*)

MOE: I hear hoofbeats. (*He pulls stethoscope out from under his robe, squats on ground and puts endpiece to floor, listening intently.*) Number twenty-one horseshoes, Army steel. That's bad. A lawman's coming. We'd best hide.

TRICKY PETE: It's too late. Get into your holiness costume. (*Lively rendition of "The Streets of Laredo" is played.* TRICKY PETE *takes off hat and coat, and* MOE, *his robe, revealing yellow monks' robes with hoods. They stow clothes in wheelbarrow and pull hoods over their heads so their faces are hidden. Sounds of close hoofbeats and of horse neighing are heard.*)

SHERIFF SAM (*From off left*): Whoa, there, whoa! (MOE *spreads canvas cover over wheelbarrow. It reads,* HOLINESS BROTHERS, TEA LEAVES READ. *As* SHERIFF SAM *enters,* TRICKY PETE *and* MOE *lower their heads and fold their hands prayerfully.*)

SHERIFF (*Removing his hat*): Pardon me, brothers. Didn't mean to interrupt the meditatin'.

TRICKY PETE (*In pious voice*): Don't give it another thought. We were almost finished. Can we be of service, Sheriff?

SHERIFF: You surely can. (*He holds up large* WANTED *poster with picture of* TRICKY PETE.) There's a ten-thousand-dollar reward for this hombre. That there is Tricky Pete Porter, the most dangerous man in the West.

MOE: Tell us about him, Sheriff.

SHERIFF (*Singing to tune of "The Streets of Laredo"*):
    Oh, Tricky Pete Porter's a master of actin',
    He's alias this and he's alias that,
    He's Russian in Reno and French in Laredo,
    He keeps his identity under his hat.

TRICKY PETE (*Speaking*): My, my. Slippery as an eel.

SHERIFF (*Continuing song*):
    He's known as a dealer in blackjack and faro,
    A seller of snake oil and nostrums is he.
    Nobody's better at badger and shell games,
    He'll skin you and win you afore you count three.

TRICKY PETE (*Shaking his head*): Oh, the wickedness of the man.

SHERIFF (*Continuing song*):
    In Cheyenne he salted a mine full of silver,
    In Denver he rustled a herd of prime beef,
    But the wickedest thing in the varmint's long record,
    Is the innocent girls he has brought to sad grief.

TRICKY PETE: Is there no end?

SHERIFF (*Continuing song*):
    He wines and he dines and he shines up to rich gals,
    He claims he's a nobleman, duke, count, or king.
    He rustles a dowry of gold from their daddies,
    And gives them a kiss and a five-and-dime ring.
    And then on the day of the poor critters' weddings,
    Whilst the band is a-thumping out "Here Comes the
        Bride,"
    He fills up his carpetbag full of their money,
    And off on a fast horse that rascal does ride.

TRICKY PETE: Scandalous. The man must be brought to

justice! How is he dressed, just in case I meet him?

SHERIFF: You keep your eyes peeled for a couple of phony foreigners. Tricky Pete always travels with an ugly little sidekick. If you run across them, get in touch with me, Circulatin' Sam, Sheriff of the six desert counties. I've got to catch those outlaws before they get wind of the windfall in New Paducah.

TRICKY PETE (*Suddenly alert*): Windfall?

SHERIFF: Big Bart Millionola, the richest man in these parts, lives in New Paducah. And he's got daughters. Yes, sir, I'm worried. Well, nice meeting you, brothers. So long. (*He exits left. Sound of hoofbeats going off is heard.* TRICKY PETE *and* MOE *pull down their cowls.*)

MOE: We've struck it rich, boss!

TRICKY PETE: Big Bart Millionola. That's the mother lode!

MOE: You are one beautiful schemer.

TRICKY PETE (*Breaking out in song, to tune of "Beautiful Dreamer"*):

Beautiful schemer, a master of guile,
I trump every heart with the charm of my smile.
Enamor young maidens, poor silly girls.
Bamboozle their bankbooks and plunder their pearls.
Watch how I woo them, with consummate skill,
Bill them and coo them, then bilk them at will.
None can resist my soft *savoir faire,*
Beautiful schemer — oh, ladies, beware!

BOTH (*Singing*):

Beautiful schemer — oh, ladies, beware!

TRICKY PETE: Come on, Gruesome Moe. Let's not keep the ladies waiting. I'm going to marry money in New Paducah! (*They exit left. A reprise of "Beautiful Dreamer" is played.*)

* * * * *

Scene 3

TIME: *Later that day.*

SETTING: *Same as Scene 1.*

AT RISE: MIKE MACADOO *stands behind bar wiping glasses.* BLANCHE *is seated at table, drinking a cherry phosphate.*

BLANCHE (*Dabbing her eyes with handkerchief*): I just don't know if I can go on in this cruel world. I lost my true love, Mr. MacAdoo, and I am desolated. Desolated!

MIKE: Yes, ma'am, Miss Blanche. That's the third true love you lost this month. Would you like another cherry phosphate to drown your sorrows?

BLANCHE: I believe I would. It'll take the edge off my misery. (MIKE *brings her another glass on tray.*) How am I to be taught the things a proper lady ought to know without a tutor? Paw is so concerned about my being brought up refined and genteel, not like some of my relatives I could name. (HORSESHOE TENNY, *wearing black suit and derby, carrying books, enters. He crosses to* BLANCHE *and bows stiffly.*)

HORSESHOE: Miss Blanche Millionola?

BLANCHE: Yes. . . .

HORSESHOE: I understand the job of tutoring is now wide open. My name is Horace Ulysses Tenny, and I am applying for the job.

BLANCHE (*Coyly*): Oh, my, oh, my. Sit right down here beside me. Why, Horace, I do believe you are the answer to a maiden's prayer. (HORSESHOE *sits beside her.*)

MIKE (*Aside*): What a name — Horace Ulysses Tenny! No wonder he calls himself Horseshoe. (*Commotion is heard from offstage.* GEEZER *bursts in through swinging door.*)

GEEZER (*Excitedly*): The Sheriff's caught Kate, and he's

bringin' her in! (*He stands near door to look out. Cow-pokes rush in.*)

CHUCKAWALLA (*Excitedly*): They're comin'! What a side-show this is goin' to be. Let's get some seats, boys. (*Cow-pokes sit on stools.* MAYOR *and* BIG BART *enter down right, and sit on bench.* KATE *is heard from offstage, protesting noisily, as* SHERIFF *backs onto stage, up right, pulling and tugging on a rope.*)

SHERIFF (*Digging in heels as if pulling a steer*): Come on, Kate. You're just making it harder on yourself.

COWPOKES (*Ad lib*): Atta boy, Sheriff! You're doin' fine! Hang on! (*Etc.* SHERIFF *gives yank and pulls* KATE *in through doors, her hands tied together and fastened to a rope. Cowpokes cheer wildly.*)

KATE: Let me go! Let me go, you slumgullyin' wonker-wackin' buzzards! Let me loose, and I'll massacre you with my bare fingernails! (BLANCHE *cringes.*)

MAYOR: Kate, you watch your language or I'll have to gag you.

KATE: You just try it and you'll have five of the shortest fingers that ever tried to deal a hand of poker.

MAYOR: Kate, we've put up with you long enough. You've brawled your last brawl in New Paducah. There's a stage leaving this morning for parts East. We're going to put you on that stage and wish you farewell forever.

COWPOKES: Hooray!

MAYOR: Rowdy Kate Millionola — I banish you from New Paducah forever.

BIG BART (*Jumping up*): No, Mayor! Wait. Don't send Katey-bird away. (TRICKY PETE, *dressed as prosperous rancher, and* MOE, *dressed as Navajo Indian, enter up right. They sit down right and watch proceedings with interest.*) My little Katey isn't a bad girl at heart. She's sweet and lovable down deep — somewhere. I believe that all she needs is a good man with a firm hand. So, gents, I am prepared to offer a dowry of one thousand dollars to any man who will marry her and settle her down. Is that a fair offer, Mayor?

MAYOR: Fair enough.

CHUCKAWALLA: A thousand dollars? Only a thousand? Do I hear two thousand, Bart?

BIG BART: All right, two thousand.

BRONC: I don't know. Two thousand is mighty small potatoes for marryin' Kate till death do you part. Do I hear five thousand, Bart?

BIG BART: But that's more money than you'd get for a herd of Holsteins! Well, make it five thousand. (*There is silence.*) Speak up, somebody. Speak up.

KATE (*Furiously*): This is the goldarnedest auction I ever heard of. Turn me loose. I refuse to be bid on like a side of beef!

BIG BART: Hush up, Kate. This is serious business.

PIGGY: Five thousand. Shucks, I'd marry a gal who looked like a polka-dot mule for five thousand, but Kate is more like one of them natural disasters. Better go to ten thousand, Bart.

BIG BART: That's a mighty big chunk of money, Piggy. Oh, well — Katey is worth it to me. (*Aside*) Getting rid of her is! (*Aloud again*) Ten thousand dollars! (*There is silence.*)

GEEZER (*Calling out*): The stage is here.

MAYOR: Come on, Kate. It's time to go.

BIG BART: Have a heart, fellers. Don't let my Katey-bird be banished. Ten thousand dollars . . .

GEEZER: Say — they've loaded up the stage. It's going . . .

MAYOR: Get on that stage, Kate. (KATE *is pulled up center by* SHERIFF.)

GEEZER: It's going . . .

TRICKY PETE (*Suddenly standing*): Sold! I'll marry Kate. (KATE *shrieks loudly.*)

GEEZER: Gone! (*All gasp, as* SHERIFF *pulls a sullen* KATE *to table, hands rope to* TRICKY PETE, *and sits.*)

BIG BART: Stranger, you are a real gent. A real gent.

MAYOR: Stranger, I hope you know what you're doing.

TRICKY PETE (*Smoothly*): To be sure. It just so happens I have been looking the town over for a nice little wife to share my ups and downs. My name's Stockman, P.J. Stockman. I'm a cattle baron in a manner of speaking, and this is my faithful Indian friend, Sitting Duck.

MOE (*Raising his hand*): How.

BIG BART: A cattle baron. Well, I couldn't ask for a more respectable occupation. When would you like to marry my Kate, Mr. Stockman?

TRICKY PETE: Tomorrow morning. Eleven o'clock sharp.

BIG BART: Tomorrow!

TRICKY PETE: What's the matter? Can't you arrange it?

COWPOKES: Yes! Yes!

MAYOR: We can arrange it. I'll waive all the red tape and make the arrangements myself.

MIKE: I'll decorate the soda parlor.

BIG BART: Mr. Stockman, I'll be pleased to hand you your certified bona fide check for ten thousand dollars right after the ceremony.

TRICKY PETE: *Before* the ceremony, if you please.

BIG BART: Anything, anything you say.

MAYOR: Folks, this is our lucky day. Now we've got to give these lovebirds a little privacy, so's they can get acquainted. Get on out, all of you. Skedaddle! (*Cowpokes and* GEEZER *exit up right.* MIKE *goes out left.* BIG BART, BLANCHE, HORSESHOE, *and* MAYOR *exit down right.* SHERIFF *takes from pocket* WANTED *poster with picture*

of TRICKY PETE, *props it up on bar, then exits right.*
TRICKY PETE *removes ropes from* KATE*'s hands, giving
ropes to* MOE, *who sits on bench, right, arms folded.*)

TRICKY PETE (*Walking around* KATE *and looking her up
and down*): Well now, what have we here?

KATE: You darn fool, you've bought yourself a pack of
trouble.

TRICKY PETE: They call you Kate, eh?

KATE: Kate the wildcat. That's what they call *me*.

TRICKY PETE: You look more like a kitty to me, Kate.
Think I'll call you Kitty. Here, Kitty. Here, Kitty. (*He
beckons to her.*)

KATE (*Swinging at him*): Watch out for my claws, stranger!

TRICKY PETE (*Ducking, then laughing*): I aim to clip your
claws, Kitty.

KATE (*Raising clenched fist*): Don't you come near me,
stranger!

TRICKY PETE: Here, Kitty, Kitty!

KATE (*Singing to tune of "Shoo, Fly, Don't Bother Me"*):
    Shoo now, don't bother me,
    Shoo now, don't bother me,
    Shoo now, don't bother me,
    For I am woolly, wild and free.
    I'm mad. I'm bad . . . I'm dangerous to know.
    I'm worse. I'm a curse. I bring bad luck and woe.

TRICKY PETE (*Continuing to sing to same tune*):
    I'll trim you down to size,
    Make you my pretty prize.
    Give up. Give in to fate.
    Seal the bargain. Kiss me, Kate!

(*He grabs* KATE *and gives her a resounding kiss.* KATE
pulls away, appalled.)

KATE: What'd you do that for? (*She slaps him hard.*)

TRICKY PETE (*Furiously*): You slapped me — me, the un-disputed king of charm! No woman ever slapped Pete Porter before. (*He pulls her to a chair, sits, turns her over his knee and spanks her.*) You've had this coming since you were in pigtails.

MOE: Give her one for me, Boss.

KATE (*Yelling*): Ow! Ow! Stop it! You can't hit me. It's against the code of the West to hit a woman.

TRICKY PETE: That so? Well, I'm from the East. (*He whacks her once more, then stands up, brushes himself off and crosses upstage.*) You. be here tomorrow morn-ing, Kate. Eleven o'clock sharp. Wear your wedding finery. Be here, or else —

KATE: Or else what?

TRICKY PETE: Or else I will hunt you down and find you and drag you by the hair of your head to this soda par-lor. (*He grins, tips his hat to her, and exits, followed by* MOE.)

KATE (*Enraged*): Oh! Oh! Oh! He kissed me. Then he whacked me. I can understand the whackin' but I can't figure out the kissin'. What'd he do it for? I'm as dizzy as a leaf in a whirlwind. (*She reels to bar and sits down, picks up* WANTED *poster and fans herself with it.*) He went and got the better of me, and I went and let him do it. (*Fans herself, then stares at poster*) What's this? Why, that's a photograph of the wily varmint! Only this poster calls him Pete Porter. (*Thoughtfully*) Pete Porter? He said no woman had ever slapped Pete Porter. But I thought his name was P.J. Stockman. (*Suddenly getting idea*) Why — he's no more P.J. Stockman than I am. He's an alias, that's what he is! What's he wanted for? (*She reads poster, growing more and more shocked with each revelation.*) Hm-m-m. Oh, no! Great balls of fire!

So that's what he's up to. (*An impish smile slowly spreads across her face.*) He wants a weddin', does he? Well, I'll give him a weddin' he'll never forget. I'm gonna give Mr. Tricky Pete Porter the weddin' of the century! (*She throws back her head and laughs heartily, as curtains close.*)

* * * * *

SCENE 4

TIME: *The next morning.*

SETTING: *Same as Scene 1, but room is refurbished, and decorated with white streamers, flowers, and wedding decorations.*

AT RISE: MIKE MACADOO, *in frock coat and vest, stands behind bar filling bowl from large sack marked* RICE. *Table down left is covered with fresh white tablecloth. There are bowl of daisies in center of table and a sign reading,* NEXT OF KIN ONLY. *Sound of excited voices is heard from offstage. Cowpokes, wearing frock coats and vests, enter through swinging door.* MAYOR *follows them in, dressed in cutaway coat and top hat, and wearing white streamer across his chest. Cowpokes stand left near barstools.* MAYOR *crosses down right.*

CHUCKAWALLA: Wahoo! You never saw such excitement out there.

BRONC: Folks have come from miles around to see Rowdy Kate get hitched.

PIGGY: Geezer's charging them fifty cents a head to park their buggies on the courthouse lawn.

CROWBAIT: They're giving odds on whether Kate is going to show up for the wedding in a pair of dirty Levi's or a pair of raggedy blue jeans.

MAYOR (*Worried*): By jinks, I hope she doesn't embarrass

the bridegroom. What about the schoolmarms? Did anybody invite the schoolmarms?

CHUCKAWALLA: We told 'em about Kate, and they were so
relieved that they volunteered to be bridesmaids.
(GEEZER *enters in his old clothes, with wilted daisy hanging out of his buttonhole.*)

GEEZER (*Breathlessly*): She's a-comin' — all wrapped up in
white, like a mummy. (*He stands by doors.*)

MAYOR (*Fretting*): That's just like Kate. The groom's not
here — her paw's not here. The wedding's not nearly
ready, and she comes trotting in. (*Calling off to musicians*) Well, play something. (GEEZER *and* MIKE *hold
doors open. "Here Comes the Bride" is played.
BLANCHE, wearing white wedding gown, her face covered
with a white veil, enters, followed by* HORSESHOE TENNY,
*dressed in ill-fitting morning coat and top hat. Almost
immediately,* PARSON EVEREADY *enters, holding book.*
BLANCHE *pushes back her veil. Music stops.*)

COWPOKES: Miss Blanche!

BLANCHE: Congratulate us, everybody. My own true love,
Mr. Horace Ulysses Tenny, and I were married this
morning. Parson Eveready married us privately in the
hotel parlor. I just couldn't bear for Kate to be the first
female Millionola to be married. Could I, Horace?

HORACE: No, ma'am, Miss Blanche.

MAYOR: Congratulations and felicitations, Miss Blanche
and Horseshoe. (*He ushers them to table.*) You sit right
down here and enjoy the show. You too, Parson. Have
a little rest between hitchings. (BLANCHE, HORSESHOE,
and PARSON EVEREADY *sit at table.* BIG BART, *his arm
around* TRICKY PETE, *enters down right.*)

BIG BART: Son, I have a small honorarium for you. This is

the ten-thousand-dollar dowry I promised you. (*He hands* TRICKY PETE *thick envelope.*)

TRICKY PETE: Much obliged, Millionola.

BIG BART: Call me Paw, son.

TRICKY PETE (*Smoothly*): Ah, yes — Paw. (*He slyly surveys room, as if looking for exit, then suddenly has fit of coughing.* BIG BART *whacks him on back, but* TRICKY PETE *pushes him aside and starts for door.*) Air! I need air. (*As he nears door,* GEEZER *blocks his way.*)

GEEZER (*Restraining him*): Too late now to go out. The bridesmaids are coming. (*"Here Comes the Bride" is played.* GEEZER *and* MIKE *hold door open, as School-marms enter, dressed as bridesmaids, in square dance skirts, ruffled blouses, and ribbons, and carrying daisy bouquets. They march solemnly downstage. Music stops.*)

MAYOR: Where is she? Where's Kate? It's just like her to be late for her own wedding.

TRICKY PETE: Allow me. I'll go fetch her. (*He heads down right.*)

BIG BART (*Pulling him back*): Don't be so impatient, young feller. It's bad luck to see your bride afore the wedding.

GEEZER: I'll go look for her. (*He exits.*)

CHUCKAWALLA: Set down, everybody. Wouldn't surprise me none if Kate has run off into the hills. (*All groan and sit down. When they are seated,* GEEZER *runs in breathlessly.*)

GEEZER: She's coming. Oh, what a sight! Wait till you see her.

MAYOR (*Moaning*): I was afraid of this.

PIGGY (*Shaking* CROWBAIT*'s hand*): Bet she's wearing Levi's.

CROWBAIT: A dollar says she's wearing blue jeans.

GEEZER (*Peering out door*): She's here.

MAYOR: Everybody rise. Here comes the bride — such as she is! (*"Here Comes the Bride" is played.* KATE *enters. All gasp and stand up, as* KATE *walks slowly forward, dressed in long, white wedding gown, a veil and tiara. Her hair hangs loose about her shoulders, and she looks scrubbed and clean. She carries white bridal bouquet, which conceals handcuffs, one half attached to her wrist, the other hanging free. She crosses center.*)

MIKE (*Awed*): That can't be Kate. Doesn't look like Kate. Doesn't walk like Kate. Doesn't act like Kate.

BIG BART: Katey-bird. It's Katey-bird! At last I've got me a daughter instead of a cow puncher. (*PARSON EVEREADY stands and crosses down left to face* KATE. *Music stops.*)

PARSON (*Lifting his hand*): Dearly beloved . . .

TRICKY PETE: Let me out of here! (KATE *grabs his hand and smiles at him dazzlingly.*)

KATE: Don't be nervous, sweetie. I aim to be a wing-ding of a wife.

PARSON: Dearly beloved, in the interests of getting these two lovebirds hitched as quickly as possible, Miss Kate has requested the short but sweet version of the wedding ceremony. Ahem. Do you, Miss Kate, take this man to be your lawful, wedded husband?

KATE: You bet! I mean, I do! (*She grabs* PETE *and kisses him hard, then swiftly clamps his wrist to hers with handcuff.* PETE *tries desperately to pull free.*)

PARSON: Whoa there, Kate. You're not supposed to kiss the groom until after he's said "I do." Ahem. Mr. P. J. Stockman, do you take Miss Kate to be your lawful, wedded wife?

KATE (*To* PETE, *in a loud whisper*): Want me to take off the handcuffs?

TRICKY PETE (*Whispering hoarsely*): Yes, I do.

PARSON: Then I now pronounce you man and wife. (*"Wedding March" is played. All applaud and cheer.* MAYOR HOBSON *waves to them to be quiet.*)

MAYOR: Ladies and gents. There's homemade punch and strawberry shortcake made by the schoolmarms, right out on the lawn. Later on, we'll serenade the lovebirds. (*Reprise of "Bill Bailey" is played, as all exit except* BLANCHE *and* HORSESHOE, KATE *and* TRICKY PETE.)

BLANCHE (*Brushing* HORSESHOE's *lapels*): Horace, there's dust all over your lapels. And do straighten your tie, dear. Are you listening, Horace? Don't just sit there like a stick, Horace. Don't you want some nice homemade punch? (*She crosses up right,* HORACE *following sheepishly.*) Horace, stand up, dear. Don't slump. (*As they exit*) Pick up your feet, Horace. You shouldn't shuffle like that.

TRICKY PETE: All right, Kate. You've had your fun with me — now unhand me!

KATE: Oh, I haven't begun to have my fun with you, Pete Porter.

TRICKY PETE: You — know?

KATE: You told me yourself. You slipped up, Pete.

TRICKY PETE: Let me go, and I'll ride out of your life.

KATE: You know what they do to men who desert their brides in this territory? They hang them. As I see it, dear husband, you have three choices: Hanging, jail, or marriage until death do us part. (*Warily*) I guess one is as bad as the other, eh?

TRICKY PETE: Hanging — jail — or marriage to Kate. Hm-m-m. (*He smiles, slowly.*) You know my reputation? You know I can charm the birds from the trees? I could be dangerous, Kate.

KATE: Could you now? Well, that makes two of us. What's it to be?

TRICKY PETE (*Looking thoughtfully at her, then reaching decision*): It's to be marriage — for better and for worse.

KATE (*Breaking into wide grin*): Fine and dandy! Let's shake on it! (*Shakes* PETE'*s free hand with hers*) Now that I've married you, I'm goin' to make an honest man out of you. Hand over Paw's bankroll, Pete! (*Reluctantly,* TRICKY PETE *hands over envelope.* KATE *waves it triumphantly over her head, as Cowpokes and Schoolmarms enter two by two through swinging door up right, and* BLANCHE, HORSESHOE, BIG BART *and* PARSON *enter down right, and* GEEZER, MIKE, MAYOR, SHERIFF *and* MOE *enter left. All stand grouped informally around* KATE *and* TRICKY PETE.)

ALL (*Singing to tune of "Bill Bailey"*):
Good times in New Paducah,
Good times today.
We're going to whoop and yell.
We'll dance around the rooftops,
We'll sing 'til dawn,
We'll ring each ding-dong bell!

MIKE (*Singing*):
I'll give free ice cream sodas,
To one and all . . .

MAYOR (*Singing*):
And I'll declare a holiday —

ALL (*Singing*):
The knot has been tied,
Rowdy Kate is a bride,
And better times are on their way . . .

MIKE (*Singing*):
In New Paducah . . .

ALL (*Singing*):
  And better times are on their way!
  (*Reprise of song is played. Cowpokes and Schoolmarms form square and dance, as others clap in rhythm to music. At end of dance, curtains close.*)

THE END

Rowdy Kate

Production Notes

Characters: 14 male; 6 female.

Playing Time: 45 minutes.

Costumes: Appropriate dress of the Old West. Cowpokes wear ragged jeans and shirts out-at-the-elbows, with shabby Stetsons; for wedding scene, they change to frock coats and vests, with clean hats, boots, and spurs. Schoolmarms wear long skirts, blouses with leg-o'-mutton sleeves, ties, and straw skimmers; for wedding, they wear square dance skirts, ruffled blouses, hair ribbons. Blanche wears ruffled, beribboned dress and carries parasol; she later wears wedding gown, veil. Kate wears black cowboy outfit, with guns; she changes to elaborate white wedding gown, tiara, and veil, and handcuffs. Tricky Pete wears astrakhan hat and Russian coat or robe over yellow monk's robe with hood; he changes to Western rancher's suit, later to appropriate wedding suit. Gruesome Moe wears turban and robe over yellow monk's robe with hood; he changes to Navajo Indian disguise of blanket, fringed buckskins, beads, feathered headband. Mayor wears WELCOME ribbon. Geezer has white whiskers. All men wear spruced-up clothes and daisies in buttonholes for wedding scene.

Properties: Banners and signs, as indicated in text; dustcloth; flyswatter; cards and poker chips; tray and glasses; prop pistols; wad of money; wheelbarrow, decorated gaudily, and reading COUNT PETRUSHKA'S MYSTIC ORIENTAL OINTMENT; canvas reading HOLINESS BROTHERS, TEA LEAVES READ; map; stethoscope; WANTED poster with photo of Tricky Pete; books; ropes; rice in sack labeled RICE; bowl; thick envelope; handcuffs, daisy bouquet.

Setting: Greasy Gulch Saloon, renamed New Pacudah Soda Parlor. There is a bar up center, with five stools in front of it. Table with chairs around it stands down left, and long bench is against wall, right. There is swinging door up right, and other exits down right and left. In Scene 1, banner painted NEW PADUCAH SODA PARLOR is draped over bar, and there are poker chips and cards on table. In Scene 4, Soda Parlor is decorated with white streamers, flowers, bells and other wedding decorations. Table is covered with white cloth. There are bowl of daisies at center of table and a sign reading, NEXT OF KIN ONLY.

Lighting: No special effects.

Sound: Hoofbeats and gunshots, as indicated in text. Live or recorded music may accompany songs. Musicians (guitar, banjo, accordion, harmonica, etc.) may be seated in orchestra, or auditorium.

CYBERNELLA

Cybernella

Space-age disco antics modeled on "Cinderella"

Characters

SCRUBBMUCH, *cleaning lady*
PETULA PEACOCK ⎫
ARROGANZA PEACOCK ⎭ *sisters*
MRS. PEACOCK, *their mother*
CYBERNELLA, *a perfect servant*
TWO DELIVERY BOYS
TICKETRONIC AGENT
WILMA WUNDERBAR, *public relations person*
BURLY BAROOM, *motorcycle stunt rider*
PHOTOGRAPHER
HERALD-HAROLD
PAGE, *a girl*
PRINCE HARMONY
TWO MEDICS
ROCK BAND
FOUR FASHION SHOW MODELS
DISCOTHEQUE FANS, *extras*
OFFSTAGE VOICES

SCENE 1

TIME: *The hazy future.*

SETTING: *The Peacocks' futuristic living room. On back wall is scribbly mural. A sofa and free-form coffee table are at center. Beanbag chairs are at right and left with end tables holding odd sculptures near them. Exit to outside is down right; exit to rest of house is down left.*

AT RISE: SCRUBBMUCH *pushes a carpet sweeper across floor, rubbing her aching back.*

PETULA (*Entering, in robe and slippers*): Scrubbmuch, bring me breakfast in bed.

ARROGANZA (*Entering, whining*): If she has her breakfast in bed, I want mine in bed, too, Scrubbmuch. Me first. (SCRUBBMUCH *grimaces and puts her fingers in her ears.* MRS. PEACOCK *enters, yawning.*)

MRS. PEACOCK (*Snapping her fingers under* SCRUBB-MUCH*'s nose*): Scrubbmuch! Listen to me. Do you hear me, Scrubbmuch? (SCRUBBMUCH *takes fingers from ears, leans on carpet sweeper resignedly as* MRS. PEA-COCK *sings a list of duties to the tune of "Battle Hymn of the Republic."*)

Oh, Scrubbmuch, make us breakfast,
And then wash and wax the floors,
Polish all the silver,
And the handles on the doors,
Dust, you must, with vigor,
In between your other chores,
The housework must go on!

PETULA (*Singing*):
Bring me squab and roasted pheasant,

ARROGANZA (*Singing*):
Brandied cherries would be pleasant,
(SCRUBBMUCH *folds her arms, balking.*)

BOTH (*Singing; militantly*):

Bring it now, you lazy peasant,
Move on, Scrubbmuch, move on!

(*As music continues,* SCRUBBMUCH *removes apron, throws it on floor, dusts hands, then faces the Peacocks defiantly.*)

SCRUBBMUCH (*Singing to the tune of "Battle Hymn of the Republic"*):

I will not make you breakfast,
And I've waxed my final floors,
I hope the tarnish varnishes
The knobs upon your doors,
I'm handing in my notice —
"Not available for chores"
Farewell, goodbye, I *quit!*

(*She runs toward Peacocks with carpet sweeper as she sings chorus, threatening to run over their feet. They yelp and dodge the sweeper.*)

Glory, glory, I am *through* here,
No more boring things to do here,
Naught to sweep or scrub or brew here,

(*Saluting each one in turn, then leaving the carpet sweeper in front of* ARROGANZA.)

Farewell — goodbye — I quit!

(SCRUBBMUCH *marches offstage, blowing a triumphant kiss at the Peacocks.*)

ARROGANZA (*In outrage*): The ingrate! That's the third maid in two days.

MRS. PEACOCK: It's all your fault, girls. You're too demanding.

PETULA: Demanding? Why, I allowed her a water break every twelve hours.

ARROGANZA: And I let her have all the leftover pet food she could eat.

MRS. PEACOCK: Never mind. I would have fired her any-

way. She was lazy. She never finished polishing the
silver, and it's only a twelve-hundred-piece set.

PETULA: But, Mother, who is going to wash my delicate
things? You don't expect me to do it, do you?

ARROGANZA: Ha! I'd like to see you lift a finger, Petula.

PETULA (*Affected*): Oh, really, Arroganza? And who lies
in bed until noon, mooning over Prince Harmony, the
great rock star at the Castle Discotheque? (*Mimicking*
ARROGANZA) "Oh, great Prince Harmony, choose little
old me to be your Princess Regent for the evening."

ARROGANZA (*Yanking* PETULA's *hair*): Keep still!

PETULA (*Wailing*): Ow! Mama, you saw that. She pulled
my hair. (*Stepping on* ARROGANZA's *foot*) Tit for tat,
you rat.

ARROGANZA (*Hopping around and howling*): Oh! Mama,
she stepped on my foot. I'll never dance again.

MRS. PEACOCK: Oh, hush, you two. Stop frowning.
You'll get wrinkles on your pretty faces. Leave it to
your mother, my pets. I have solved the servant problem.

PETULA: How, I'd like to know? No agency has sent us a
maid since that silly thing jumped out the window.

MRS. PEACOCK: Science has come to our rescue, my dears.

ARROGANZA: What does that mean, Mama?

MRS. PEACOCK: It means that very shortly we will acquire
a perfect servant.

PETULA: There's no such thing. The minute they come to
our house they have nervous breakdowns and ulcers.

MRS. PEACOCK: That's because they're only human. You
just wait and see, girls. (*Knock at door*) Ah, that's the
new maid now. (*She crosses downstage right.* CYBER-
NELLA, *a large delivery tag tied to her hand, and a bag
stamped* FRAGILE, HANDLE WITH CARE *over her head,*

is wheeled in on dolly by TWO DELIVERY BOYS. *She wears maid's uniform and transparent galoshes.*) Bring her in carefully. I paid a lot for her.

1ST BOY (*Producing pad and pencil*): One perfect servant. Sign here, please. (MRS. PEACOCK *signs.*)

2ND BOY (*Handing* MRS. PEACOCK *manual*): Your instruction book, ma'am. (BOYS *put their hands out to* MRS. PEACOCK *expectantly. She shakes each hand.*)

MRS. PEACOCK: Thank you very much, boys. Goodbye. (*She points to exit right.* BOYS, *shaking heads, cross downstage.*)

1ST BOY: Did you see that? A handshake instead of a tip.

2ND BOY: Yeah. Did you see those girls? Their faces would stop a clock.

1ST BOY: Yeah. Big Ben. (*They exit.* MRS. PEACOCK *takes bag off* CYBERNELLA's *head, revealing young woman in a maid's uniform.* MRS. PEACOCK *hands manual to* PETULA.)

MRS. PEACOCK: This is our new maid. A robot just off the assembly line from Perfect Servants, Inc. Petula, make yourself useful by reading the manual of instructions.

PETULA: Why do I have to do all the dirty work? Why can't Arroganza read the booklet? (*She hands booklet to* ARROGANZA.)

ARROGANZA: Me? Oh, all right. (*Reading*) "You have just purchased your first perfect servant. She is model 14372, a voice-activated robot maid, code named Cybernella."

MRS. PEACOCK: Yes, you see, in order to start her you need only speak her name. (*Loudly*) Cybernella — speak.

CYBERNELLA (*Standing stiffly and speaking mechanically*):

Good morning, madam. (*She curtsies with a jerk.*)

MRS. PEACOCK (*Delighted*): She's working! Uh — Cybernella, have a nice day.

CYBERNELLA: Thank you, madam. The same to you.

PETULA: My turn. Cybernella, sit up and beg. (CYBERNELLA *crouches and begs like a puppy.*) Ha, ha! Cybernella, roll over. (CYBERNELLA *lies down and rolls over.*)

ARROGANZA: You nincompoop! She's a maid, not a trained poodle. Let me try her. Cybernella, clean the room. (CYBERNELLA *runs to carpet sweeper and runs back and forth with it as girls applaud.*)

MRS. PEACOCK: Stop. That's enough, Cybernella. Don't wear out your switches. (CYBERNELLA *stops instantly.*)

ARROGANZA: Why, she really is perfect. Listen to this. (*Reading on*) "Cybernella is programmed to do the hundred-and-one household chores humans find so humdrum. Cybernella will work tirelessly and efficiently, without the need for food, rest or a salary. She will never steal your silver, eat your filet mignon, demand a raise or give notice. She will instantly obey *anyone* who activates her vibratory mechanism."

PETULA: But is she guaranteed? What's she made of, anyway?

ARROGANZA (*Reading*): "Cybernella is guaranteed for a lifetime of service. She is composed of germanium transistors, titanium wires, platinum gears, sugar, spice and everything nice. You will notice that she wears glass ~~galoshes~~ *shoes* in order to reduce the shock hazard to her owners." (*Knock at door is heard.* PETULA *starts down right.*) Let Cybernella answer that, you dummy. That's what she's here for.

PEACOCKS (*Together*): Cybernella, answer the door. (CY-

BERNELLA *runs down right, admitting* TICKETRONIC
AGENT, *bobbing curtsy and pulling him through door.*)

CYBERNELLA (*Singing to tune of "Bill Bailey, Won't You
Please Come Home"*):
Won't you come in? You're welcome!
Won't you come in?
We're happy you're our guest.
(*Removing his coat and hat*)
I'll take your coat and hat, sir,
I'll make you tea,
Madam will be impressed.
(*Bobs curtsy, pushes* AGENT *to sofa, forces his head
down on pillow, props his feet up on sofa arm, remov-
ing shoes as she sings*)
Make yourself comfy-cozy,
Put up your feet,
And have a nice, relaxing rest,
If there's something you need,
Just call, and I'll heed,
For, Cybernella, she knows best,
Oh, yes, indeedy,
Cybernella, she knows best.

TICKET AGENT (*As he puts on shoes, protesting*): No, no.
You don't understand. Listen — I'm only a ticket
agent. (*Stands*) Miss Arroganza Peacock? Special delivery ticket to the Castle Discotheque for a concert by
Prince Harmony. Sign here. (ARROGANZA *signs quickly,
takes envelope, removes ticket.* AGENT *puts out hand
expectantly.* ARROGANZA *hands him empty envelope.*
PETULA *blocks his exit.*)

PETULA (*Furious*): Oh! She got tickets to the concert tonight. She never said a word to me. The Prince Harmony concert. He's going to choose a girl to sit on the

bandstand with him and be his Princess Regent for the evening. All the Hollywood and Broadway stars and the international jet set will be there, in the latest fashions. I want to go too! Mama, tell her she can't go without me. (*She screams.*) Do you hear me, Mama?

MRS. PEACOCK (*Soothingly*): There, love, my precious. Of course baby Petula shall go. (*To* AGENT) Have you any more tickets to the concert?

AGENT: Only two left, and they're a hundred apiece.

MRS. PEACOCK: I'll take them. Charge them to the Peacocks.

AGENT (*Handing her tickets*): Yes, ma'am. (*Exits*)

ARROGANZA: Two tickets? It's bad enough that Petula is going. Who's the other ticket for?

MRS. PEACOCK: For me, sweetie. After all, I have to keep an eye on my precious darlings, don't I?

PETULA *and* ARROGANZA (*Groaning*): Oh, Mother! You're really out of it! (*Curtain*)

* * * * *

SCENE 2

TIME: *That evening.*

SETTING: *The same as Scene 1. The carpet sweeper has been removed.*

AT RISE: CYBERNELLA, *dust cloth in hand, runs about room dusting coffee table and sculptures.* PETULA *enters in her "best" clothes — patched overalls and football jersey and construction boots. She sits on sofa, stretching out her feet.*

PETULA: Cybernella, you clunk, tie my shoelaces. (CYBERNELLA *drops dust cloth, crosses to* PETULA *and begins to tie laces.* ARROGANZA *enters wearing ragged jeans, gar-*

ish polo shirt and thick-soled shoes, and holding out hairbrush.)

ARROGANZA: Never mind her, Cybernella. Come here and do my hair. (CYBERNELLA *runs to* ARROGANZA, *brushing her hair rapidly.)*

PETULA: Come back here, Cybernella. You haven't finished my shoelaces. (CYBERNELLA *rushes to* PETULA, *tying her shoelaces together.)*

ARROGANZA: I had her first, Petula. Cybernella — brush! (CYBERNELLA *returns to* ARROGANZA, *brushing so hard the brush gets completely tangled in her hair.)* Ow! You stupid robot. You've tangled the brush in my hair.

PETULA (*Rising and pointing derisively at* ARROGANZA): Ha-ha! You'll never get the brush out. You'll have to meet Prince Harmony with a brush stuck in your hair. (*She starts forward, but stumbles.)* Oh! Cybernella, you hunk of junk — you've tied my shoelaces together.

PETULA *and* ARROGANZA (*Wailing*): Mama! (MRS. PEACOCK *enters in "evening" attire — a football warm-up suit with battered sneakers and a crushed painter's cap.)*

MRS. PEACOCK: Girls, girls, don't scowl, you'll get wrinkles. (*Admiring them*) My, don't you look stylish. The last word in fashion. Prince Harmony won't be able to resist you. (*Preening*) How do you like my outfit?

PETULA: Divine! Where did you get it? The Salvation Army?

MRS. PEACOCK: Yes, of course. Doesn't everybody? Well, shall we be on our way?

ARROGANZA: Let's go. (*As she crosses to door,* PETULA *scoots along beside her.)* Oh, no. I'm not walking with her.

MRS. PEACOCK: Now, darlings. (*Getting between them*)

One beauty on this side. One on the other. Why, when Prince Harmony sees you two, he'll think you are absolutely far away.

ARROGANZA: Far *out,* Mama. Can't you get anything right?

MRS. PEACOCK: Come along, girls. Oh — Cybernella. While we are away, clean up the bedrooms, wax the kitchen floor, hand-launder the linen, and put all the books in alphabetical order.

CYBERNELLA (*Curtsying*): Yes, madam. Anything else?

MRS. PEACOCK: Not at the moment. But I'll think of something when I get home.

CYBERNELLA: Yes, madam. Have a pleasant evening. (*As they exit,* PETULA *turns.*)

PETULA: Cybernella! So long, you wind-up toy! (*Sticks out her tongue at* CYBERNELLA)

CYBERNELLA (*Curtsying again*): Thank you, madam, and the same to you. (*She returns to dusting. There is a knock at door.* CYBERNELLA *crosses right, admitting* WILMA WUNDERBAR *accompanied by* PHOTOGRAPHER, *and* BURLY BAROOM, *who carries large box.*)

WILMA: Congrats, congrats, congrats! You have just opened the door to fame and fortune.

CYBERNELLA (*Bobbing*): Good evening, madam. Who shall I say is calling?

WILMA: Oh, isn't she quaint, quaint, quaint? You may say Wilma Wunderbar is calling. I am the public relations person from the world-famous Good Fairy Boutique, where the elite meet and greet. You lucky duck. You are the one-thousandth person to answer your doorbell. What's your name, dearie?

CYBERNELLA: Cybernella, madam.

WILMA: Cybernella, you are going to be the envy of the

entire female population of the entire world. (*Singing to the tune of "Ta-ra-ra-boom-de-ay"*)

Tonight you're going to a bash,

And you're going to be a smash,

BURLY (*Singing*):

Harmony will be the host

You, the maiden with the most.

WILMA (*Singing*):

Your wardrobe's going to shriek with chic,

"Good Fairy" will be your boutique!

You will be the latest rage,

Splashed on every fashion page.

BURLY (*Singing chorus*):

To make the scene's my goal,

My Harley's revved to roll,

Get on the handlebars,

We'll buzz the moon and Mars!

WILMA (*Speaking*): Wait! Show her the goodies, Burly. (*Music vamps while* WILMA *speaks.* BURLY *takes lid from box he carries.* WILMA *holds up garments inside.*) There. Isn't it breathtaking? A simulated set of World War II fatigues from a private first-class in the motor pool.

BURLY: *And,* you get a personal escort. *Me,* Burly Baroom, the stunt rider who drove his wheels up the side of Mt. Everest and jumped the whole kingdom of Nepal! (*Singing to tune of "Ta-ra-ra-boom-de-ay"*)

To make the scene's my goal,

My Harley's revved to roll,

Get on the handlebars,

We'll buzz the moon and Mars.

(*Speaking*) Come on, Cybernella, baby. Get with it. Let's split.

WILMA: Just a minute, Cybernella. Hold the cycle, Burly. The clothes you'll be wearing — they've already been sold to a rich maharani in Hindustan. You can only have them until twelve o'clock. So you must be out of the Castle Discotheque on the stroke of twelve, or you'll be repossessed on the spot. Understand?

CYBERNELLA: Oh, yes, madam. I compute.

WILMA: She *computes.* Isn't she adorable? Come on, let's get out the press releases. (*As they exit,* BURLY *hands* CYBERNELLA *the box.*)

BURLY: Say, Cybernella, do you want to ride on the seat or the handlebars? (*Quick curtain*)

*   *   *   *   *

SCENE 3

TIME: *Later that evening.*

SETTING: *The interior of the Castle Discotheque. A raised platform with two thrones and band instruments is up center. Behind it is tapestry with sign reading* CASTLE DISCOTHEQUE.

AT RISE: *At left and right are low tables with pillows, tuffets, and rugs, on which recline* DISCOTHEQUE FANS. *Down left at entrance stands* PAGE, *a girl.* ARROGANZA, PETULA *and* MRS. PEACOCK *enter.* PAGE *stops them.*

PAGE: Halt! Who goeth there, fie or forsooth?

PETULA (*Holding out tickets*): Stop fie-ing and forsoothing. We have tickets.

ARROGANZA: Is she for real?

MRS. PEACOCK: She's atmosphere, girls, just atmosphere. I'll handle her. (*Barging past* PAGE) Let's take those pillows up front. (PAGE *bars her way.*)

PAGE: Full house. You taketh what you getteth, and you getteth three small scatter rugs at the back of the house.

(*She leads them down right.*)

PETULA: Way back here? Prince Harmony will never see us back here.

ARROGANZA: I'm not sitting on any little bitty scatter rug.

PAGE: Taketh it or leaveth it. Shouldst I call the sheriff?

MRS. PEACOCK: Don't call the sheriff, for heaven's sake. Come on, girls. I'll complain to the manager later. (*They sit down right.* ROCK BAND, *dressed as knights, enters. Drummer gives a drum roll. Colored spotlight plays on bandstand.* HERALD-HAROLD, *dressed as court jester in Groucho mask, walking like Groucho, enters.*)

HERALD-HAROLD: Hey nonny nonny and scooby-dooby-doo. Good evening, fans. This is your court jester Herald-Harold with a smile, a song and a soft buskin.

FANS (*Ad lib*): Boo. Bring on Prince Harmony. (*Etc.*)

HERALD-HAROLD: But before we bring on Prince Harmony, have you heard this one? Why does a dragon cross the road?

FANS (*Clapping; in rhythm*): We want Harmony. We want Harmony.

HERALD-HAROLD: Who doesn't want Harmony? Listen, you're going to love this one. Why does the King wear red suspenders?

FANS (*Rising and making fists*): Boo! Boo!

HERALD-HAROLD: All right, all right. I can take a hint. And now — without further ado, here he comes, that rajah of rhythm, your favorite rock star and mine, the one, the only, the original — Prince Harmony! (PRINCE HARMONY *enters, in royal robes, wearing sunglasses and a crown, and thumping a tambourine.* BAND *gives him a fanfare.* FANS *scream and applaud.* HERALD-HAROLD *sings to the tune of "Shortnin' Bread" chorus*)

Ev'rybody get down, turn around, line up,

Time to meet the Monarch of Melody,
Ev'ry li'l girlie loves the Royal Rocker,
Ev'ry li'l girlie loves Harmony.

1ST FAN (*Singing to the tune of "Shortnin' Bread" verse*):
He's so outrageous!

2ND FAN (*Singing*):
He's just a fox!

3RD FAN (*Singing*):
Catch him on the downbeat,

4TH FAN (*Singing*):
Put him in a box!

5TH FAN (*Waving astrology book at* PRINCE; *singing*):
Look — we're *fated,*
Both Gemini,
We're star-mated,
You and I. Ooh! (*She faints. Music vamps.*)

HERALD-HAROLD (*Speaking*): Medics! Medics! (TWO
MEDICS *enter with stretcher and bear* 5TH FAN *offstage
left.*) Don't panic. It's nothing serious — just an acute
case of rapture. We have a full staff of rapture special-
ists on duty at all times, so feel free to faint. It's on the
house. And now, it's time for the Grand Review. Prince
Harmony himself will look you over. One, and only one
of you will be invited to sit on the royal throne and
thump the royal tambourine.

FANS (*Singing to tune of "Shortnin' Bread" chorus*):
Ev'rybody, get down, turn around, line up,
Here comes the Monarch of Melody,
Ev'ry li'l girlie loves the Royal Rocker,
Ev'ry li'l girlie loves Harmony.

HERALD-HAROLD (*Speaking*): And here to introduce our
galaxy of glittering girlies is a public-relations person

from the Good Fairy Boutique — Wilma Wunderbar.
(FANS *applaud as* WILMA *enters from up right to a drum roll.*)

WILMA: Greetings, greetings, greetings from The Good Fairy Boutique. Oh, wowee-wow, I see stars from Hollywood, high society and the international jet set here tonight, and they're competing to catch the eye of Prince Harmony. (*Catchy, disco version of "The Merry Widow Waltz" is played.*) There's the music, and here come the dancing dreamboats in the latest fashions. Say — isn't that *the* Tiffany Astor, wearing a Givenchy original? (1ST MODEL *enters and dances by platform, shaking maracas, and wearing a Mexican peon costume.*) What a fashion scoop! Tiffany Astor has outdone herself in an unbleached cotton Mexican peon outfit. (*She exits.* 2ND MODEL *enters wearing Chinese coolie outfit. As she dances by, she makes an Oriental bow to* PRINCE HARMONY, *who stifles a yawn.*) Will you look at that! Tiffany Astor's arch rival, Tiffany Vanderbilt, has outbid her with a Pucci original. Debutante Vanderbilt is making the scene with an Oriental flair as a Chinese coolie. (3RD MODEL *dances by, in costume of a beggar, barefoot. She holds out begging bowl to* PRINCE HARMONY, *who shrugs and looks bored.*) Oh, I don't believe it! Here's Hollywood's top glamour girl, Tiffany Tuesday, in a breathtaking Hollywood creation. Tiffany is absolutely ravishing as a beggar. Her bowl is a genuine Burmese begging bowl and she has that stylish barefoot look. (4TH MODEL, *dressed as chimney sweep, with broom and blackened face, dances by, shyly sweeping* PRINCE HARMONY's *feet.*) Oh, wowee-wow, fashion history is being made tonight. Here she comes,

the radiant Duchess of Sandwich-on-Rye, a leading
member of the international jet set, Lady Tiffany Twig-
gingham, and she's sporting the outfit of a Victorian
chimney sweep. How chic! And look, she's trying to
sweep Prince Harmony off his feet. (PRINCE HARMONY
steps away, disdainfully.) Oh, marvy, marvy, marvy.
Isn't this heaven? I can't remember when I've seen such
an array of faded jeans, scruffy combat boots, and
patched patches. Why, one outfit is more gloriously
tacky than the next. (*Music stops. There is a fanfare.*)
Oh-h-h. There's the fanfare. Prince Harmony is about
to make his selection. (*Offstage sound of motorcycle
roaring is heard.*) No, wait. Is that a motorcycle I hear?
(CYBERNELLA, *dressed in army fatigues, enters down
left, on the arm of* BURLY BAROOM. *She wears a cap
pulled low over her eyes.* PRINCE HARMONY *gapes at
her.*)

PRINCE HARMONY: Oh, wowee-wow. Far-out. She's so far
out she's out of sight. Oh, man!

WILMA: Fantastic! It's a mystery guest brought here special delivery by Burly Baroom. (BURLY *waves as* FANS
cheer, then retires to side, waiting.) The mystery guest is
wearing a Good Fairy original — a genuine, simulated
army-fatigue uniform. And listen, girls, tomorrow this
same uniform will be on sale at Good Fairy Boutique
for only $19.99 plus tax. ("*Merry Widow Waltz,*" in
disco tempo, begins again. CYBERNELLA *dances.* PRINCE
HARMONY *follows every movement, then joins her on
dance floor.*)

PRINCE HARMONY (*Singing to tune of "Merry Widow
Waltz"*):
    You're a classy little lassie,
    Stay a while,

I like your well-constructed chassis,
Like your style.
If you stick with me, babe,
We can make the scene,
I've got great connections, chick,
To crown you Queen.

CYBERNELLA (*Singing*):
Sir, good evening.
Well, how are you?
Have a seat.
How's the weather?
Tell me whether
You will eat?
May I get you coffee?
May I take your hat?
Would you like to sit a while,
And have a chat?

PRINCE HARMONY (*Speaking*): Oh, wowee-wow! What a cool chick! (*He throws himself into a fast disco dance, which CYBERNELLA mimics. At finish, she curtsies.*)

PETULA (*Suspiciously*): That mystery guest reminds me of someone. (PRINCE HARMONY *holds up his hand.* HERALD-HAROLD *motions* WILMA *aside. She joins* BURLY.)

HERALD-HAROLD (*Imitating fanfare*): Ta-da-de-um-de-dum. Ladies and fans. His royal heigh-de-ho-ness has an announcement to make. (FANS *cheer.*)

PETULA: Wait! He can't make an announcement.

ARROGANZA: He hasn't seen us yet.

HERALD-HAROLD: Quiet, or I'll call the sheriff. Prince Harmony can make an announcement —

FANS: Any time he wants to!

HERALD-HAROLD: Right. And now, without further ado, an announcement from Prince Harmony.

PRINCE HARMONY: I —

HERALD-HAROLD: Yes, Prince Harmony, that serene highness of serenades.

PRINCE HARMONY: I —

HERALD-HAROLD: That monarch of minstrelsy, that sovereign of song, that — (PRINCE HARMONY *claps his hand over* HERALD-HAROLD*'s mouth.*)

PRINCE HARMONY: I have chosen.

GIRLS (*Breaking into song to the tune of Handel's "Hallelujah Chorus"*): He has chosen. He has chosen. Hallelujah. Hallelujah. Hal-le-lu-jah!

1ST GIRL: Who — who — who stole your heart away?

2ND GIRL: Tell us. Oh, I'm *dying!*

HERALD-HAROLD: Fainting only. No dying. Who?

FANS (*Singing to tune of "Shortnin' Bread" verse*):
Who's got the Prince?
Who can it be?
Who stole the heart of
Har-mo-ny?

PETULA (*Clasping heart; singing*):
I'm all a-flutter,
It must be *me* —

ARROGANZA (*Singing*):
No, *I've* caught the fancy of
Har-mo-ny.

FANS (*Singing*):
Who's the littlewhosit who's hooked our hero?
The mystery miss with the magic power?
What's her name and where does she come from?
The maid of the moment and the man of the hour!
(*They lift their arms to* PRINCE HARMONY, *appealing.*)

PRINCE HARMONY (*Crossing to* CYBERNELLA *and holding*

up her hand): The winner! (*All gasp, applaud and cheer. Sound of clock striking twelve is heard.*)

WILMA (*Calling out to* CYBERNELLA): Twelve o'clock, duckie. Time to go.

BURLY (*Grabbing* CYBERNELLA *and running down left*): Come on, you've got to split. I only put a nickel in the meter. (PRINCE HARMONY *makes a flying tackle at* CYBERNELLA, *catching her foot and wrenching off a glass galosh.* CYBERNELLA, *pulled by* BURLY, *hops offstage. Motorcycle sound is heard.*)

PRINCE HARMONY (*Calling after her*): Wait! Haven't I seen you somewhere? It seems to me we have met before. But who knows where or when? (*Holding up galosh, puzzled*) What's this? ~~Good gosh~~ — a glass *shoe* ~~galosh~~! (*Quick curtain.* BAND *may take places in front of curtain and play selections until next scene is set.*)

* * * * *

SCENE 4

TIME: *A week later.*

SETTING: *The same as Scene 1.*

AT RISE: PETULA *is draped languidly on sofa, doing her nails.* MRS. PEACOCK *perches on arm of sofa, reading newspaper.* ARROGANZA, *her hair in curlers, enters down left. All three are in robes and slippers.*

ARROGANZA (*To* PETULA): Get up, you lazy thing. You can't have the whole sofa to yourself. Mama, tell her she can't have the whole sofa to herself.

PETULA: I got here first. Mama, tell her I got here first.

MRS. PEACOCK: Girls, girls. I can't hear myself think. (*Putting down paper and sighing*) The paper is full of nothing but that mystery guest. Why, Prince Harmony has put a full-page ad in the paper to find that girl!

And he's personally trying her glass ~~galosh~~ shoe on every female in the city.

ARROGANZA (*Thoughtfully*): A glass galosh. I wish I could remember where I heard about glass galoshes. (*Knock at door is heard.*)

PEACOCKS: Cybernella! (CYBERNELLA, *back in maid's uniform, runs in, wearing one glass galosh, to admit* HERALD-HAROLD *and* PRINCE HARMONY. HERALD-HAROLD *holds glass galosh on a tray.*)

CYBERNELLA (*Bobbing*): Good morning, sirs. Who shall I say is calling, sir? (PEACOCKS *rise, astonished.*)

PEACOCKS: Prince Harmony!

MRS. PEACOCK: Oh, my heavens! Oh, dear me! Pray excuse our dishabille. Had we but known you would arrive so soon, we would have dressed more appropriately.

HERALD-HAROLD: Keep your lid on, lady. Prince Harmony is not here for a fashion show. He's here to find the owner of a glass galosh.

PETULA (*Fluttering her eyelashes at* PRINCE HARMONY): A glass galosh? What a funny coincidence. I just happened to lose one. It's mine. (*She grabs galosh, trying to cram it on.*)

HERALD-HAROLD: I've got an even funnier coincidence. Half the girls in town say they lost a glass galosh. Take it off. It doesn't fit. (ARROGANZA *grabs galosh from* PETULA*'s foot.*)

ARROGANZA: Of course it doesn't fit. It's mine. (*She tugs and pulls, huffing and puffing.*)

HERALD-HAROLD (*Quizzically*): That's a foot? It looks more like a yard to me. (PETULA *howls with laughter.*)

ARROGANZA: Well, it fit last week. My foot must have swelled with the heat.

HERALD-HAROLD: What heat? It's snowing out there. (*He*

pulls galosh off her foot.) Any more customers?

MRS. PEACOCK: No one. But please — won't you let them try again? Perhaps with a little butter on the toes.

PRINCE HARMONY (*Gazing at* CYBERNELLA): Who's the little mouse? How about letting her try on the galosh? shoe

PEACOCKS (*Screaming with laughter*): Cybernella?

MRS. PEACOCK: You must be joking. Don't you know what she is?

ARROGANZA: Cybernella? A glass galosh? shoe Oh-oh! I re-member where I read about glass galoshes. shoes (*Barking an order*) Cybernella, go to the kitchen. Double time. Triple time. (CYBERNELLA *starts to run to kitchen.*)

PRINCE HARMONY: Cybernella — halt! (CYBERNELLA *freezes instantly, one foot in the air.* PRINCE HARMONY *slips galosh on the foot. Offstage fanfare.*) It fits!

OFFSTAGE VOICES (*Singing to tune of "Hallelujah Cho-rus"*): Hallelujah. Hallelujah. Hal-le-lu-jah!

HERALD-HAROLD: Oh, man, at last. I feel like a podiatrist after a marathon. I never want to see another foot again.

MRS. PEACOCK: One moment, if you please. We wouldn't want you to take this creature on false pretenses, would we, girls?

PETULA *and* ARROGANZA (*Smiling smugly and nodding to each other*): Oh, no.

MRS. PEACOCK: I think it is only fair to tell you that Cybernella is a cleverly constructed — *robot.*

PETULA *and* ARROGANZA (*Jeering*): A robot — nyaah!

HERALD-HAROLD: A robot?

PETULA: That's right. She's a mechanical mess, full of gears and wires and nasty old transistors.

ARROGANZA: She hasn't got a human bone in her inhuman body.

PRINCE HARMONY: Is she — is she Model 14372?

MRS. PEACOCK: Why, yes.

PRINCE HARMONY: Cybernella, don't you remember me? The laboratory — the assembly line. Compute, Cybernella, compute.

MRS. PEACOCK: What is this? How can Prince Harmony possibly know a creature like Cybernella?

ARROGANZA: He's so unreal.

HERALD-HAROLD: Right! Haven't you ever wondered how Prince Harmony could please all of the women all of the time? He's far out because he's an experimental model. And he's unreal — because he's unreal. He's prototype number 7717-90565 — the perfect musician.

PETULA: Oh, no!

CYBERNELLA: I compute, Prince Harmony. You were being assembled at the same time I was being assembled. We were robots that passed in the night.

PRINCE HARMONY: Cybernella, will you cross wires with me?

CYBERNELLA (*Curtsying*): Oh, yes, sir. (*He kisses her.*)

HERALD-HAROLD: And they both lived electronically ever after.

PETULA (*In a rage*): It isn't fair! What about us?

ARROGANZA: Yes, what about us? In every version of this blasted fairy tale, we're always the losers.

MRS. PEACOCK: Girls, girls. I'll think of something. (*With sudden inspiration*) Oh, Harold —

HERALD-HAROLD: Yes?

MRS. PEACOCK: What are you doing tonight? (PETULA *and* ARROGANZA *surround* HERALD-HAROLD, *smiling.* CYBERNELLA *and* PRINCE HARMONY *cross down center, as other cast members re-enter for finale.* CYBERNELLA and PRINCE *sing duet, to chorus of "Merry Widow Waltz" disco style*)

CYBERNELLA *and* PRINCE HARMONY (*Singing to tune of "Merry Widow Waltz"*):
We'll cross wires and spark together,
Hand in glove,
Automated, regulated,
Perfect love,

CYBERNELLA (*Singing*):
You are so magnetic —

PRINCE HARMONY (*Singing*):
I get my charge from you —

BOTH (*Singing*):
Together we'll compute the root
Of love so true.

ALL (*Joining in final chorus, then performing disco dance as curtains close*):
Cybernella's got her fella,
After all.
What a scene — it's wild and crazy,
What a ball!
Get down for Boogie,
Time for romance,
Get down for Disco now,
And dance, dance, dance!

(*Disco dance as curtain closes.*)

THE END

Cybernella

PRODUCTION NOTES

Characters: 9 male; 11 female; female extras for Fans, Offstage Voices; male and female extras for Rock Band.

Playing Time: 30 minutes.

Costumes: Cybernella wears maid's black uniform and transparent galoshes, except in Scene 3, where she wears army fatigues and cap. Peacocks wear robes and slippers in Scenes 1 and 4, and ragged jeans, T-shirts, etc., in Scenes 2 and 3, as described in text. Prince Harmony wears crown, cloak, hose and doublet and sunglasses. Band are dressed as knights. Page and Herald-Harold wear appropriate costumes; Harold wears Groucho mask. Delivery Boys, Ticketronic Agent, Medics wear appropriate uniforms. Burly has on motorcycle jacket. Wilma wears flashy pantsuit. Photographer wears suit. Scrubbmuch wears old housedress, white wig, apron. Fashion Show Models are dressed as described in text, and Fans wear jeans, T-shirts, etc. Makeup and hair should be weird and futuristic.

Properties: Carpet sweeper; delivery tag; bag stamped "Fragile, handle with care"; dolly; instruction manual; envelope with tickets; dust cloth; brush; box containing army fatigues; tambourine; newspaper; tray.

Setting: Scenes 1, 2, and 4: The Peacocks' futuristic living room. There is a scribbly mural on the back wall, and a sofa and free-form coffee table are at center. Beanbag chairs are at right and left, with end tables holding pieces of odd sculpture near them. Exit to outside is down right, exit to rest of house is down left. Scene 3: The Castle Discotheque. Two thrones and band instruments are on platform up center. Tapestry on back wall has futuristic sign reading CASTLE DISCOTHEQUE. Left and right of bare center stage area are low tables with pillows, tuffets, and scatter rugs around them. Exit down left leads to outside, exit at right to rest of Discotheque.

Lighting: Colored spotlight in Scene 3, as indicated in text.

Sound: Motorcycle, rock music, clock chiming twelve, fanfare, drum roll, as indicated in text. Live or recorded music may accompany songs, and, in Scene 3, Rock Band may perform live music, or they may pantomime while recorded music is played offstage.

THE TOWN THAT COULDN'T WAKE UP

The Town That Couldn't Wake Up

Romantic melodrama that retells "Sleeping Beauty"

Characters

SHERIFF BOYD BLUEBONNET
AMANDA BLUEBONNET, *his wife*
LARK BLUEBONNET, *their daughter*
CORA LEE HOOPWELL, *the schoolmarm*
DOC SAWYER
GAL SAL, *hotel proprietress*
GRANNY CONJURE, *apothecary witch-woman*
BADPENNY, *a villain*
CHIEF THOUSAND-FEATHERS
BY-GOSH MCQUADE, *a prospector*
WING DING LEE, *chef*
LONGHORN JIM GARRISON, *territorial governor*
JOHNNY THOUSAND-FEATHERS
TOM LAWRENCE
TWO CAVALRY TROOPERS
FOUR COWBOYS
THE BARBED WIRE GANG, *four outlaws*
OFFSTAGE VOICE
TOWNSPEOPLE, *extras*

SCENE 1

TIME: *Frontier days; a spring morning.*

SETTING: *Main Street, in a raw, new frontier outpost called Potluck, in the Arizona Territory. A hotel with a swinging door is at center. Sign on hotel reads:* GAL SAL'S FAMILY HOTEL. *Another sign says:* CUISINE BY CANTON CHEF WING DING. GENTEEL DANCING WITH WHITE GLOVES EVERY SATURDAY EVENING. *Western stores with signs are on either side of the hotel;* BY-GOSH MCQUADE'S HONEST ASSAY PARLOR *and* DOC SAWYER'S HORSE AND HUMAN MEDICAL OFFICE. *A sign in the doctor's window reads:* GRANNY CONJURE'S HERBS AND POTIONS. WARTS CURED. FREE ADVICE TO THE LOVELORN. *A speaker's stand is at right center, hung with bunting and a banner that says:* POTLUCK WELCOMES GOVERNOR LONGHORN JIM. *Piano is nearby.*

AT RISE: CORA LEE HOOPWELL *is seated at piano, playing, with flourishes, "There'll Be a Hot Time in the Old Town Tonight" (or pantomiming to recorded music).* TOWNSPEOPLE, GAL SAL, GRANNY CONJURE, BOYD BLUEBONNET, BY-GOSH MCQUADE, WING DING LEE, *carrying a huge plate of spareribs, and* CHIEF THOUSAND-FEATHERS, *with parchment scroll in hand, are onstage. Others sing, but* CHIEF *folds arms and remains silent.*

ALL (*Singing, to tune of "There'll Be a Hot Time in the Old Town Tonight"*):
When you hear those bugles bally-hoo,
There's going to be a great big whoop-de-doo,
And when the fanfare's through, we'll shout "Halle-
loo!"
There'll be a hot time in Potluck tonight!

GAL SAL (*Singing*):

    Grand promenade, strut up the street and down!

GRANNY (*Singing*):

    Rockets in the sky —

BOYD (*Singing*):

    And torches in the town.

CORA LEE (*Singing; from the piano*):

    Singing till the dawn —

WING DING (*Bowing and singing*):

    And spareribs nice and brown,

ALL (*Singing*):

    There'll be a hot time in Potluck tonight.

    Combustion in Potluck tonight.

    Oh, yes, a whiz-bang in Potluck . . . *tonight!*

(*All shout*) Halle-loo!

BOYD (*Stepping forward to quiet them down*): Folks, folks!

GAL SAL: We hear you, Brother Bluebonnet.

BOYD: As you know very well, our little old crossroads is about to become a real, live *town*.

BY-GOSH: You tell 'em, Sheriff Bluebonnet!

CORA LEE (*From piano*): Amen. A town. With a schoolhouse and young'uns for me to teach readin' and writin' and 'rithmetic.

GAL SAL: A town. Elegant folk coming by stage coach to *my* hotel. And me saying, "Welcome to Potluck."

WING DING (*Grinning and bowing*): Many, many customers for Wing Ding Lee, Master of All Chefs, from Hong Kong.

GRANNY: Young folks'll be striking out on their own. There'll be moonstruck sweethearts making calves' eyes at each other. And they'll come to old Granny Conjure for love potions.

BY-GOSH: Miners with gold and silver will come to town. And, by gosh, I'll be assaying those nuggets!

THOUSAND-FEATHERS: Double trade in beads and blankets for my tribe.

BOYD: You bet! Why, we'll have us a boom town. In no time there'll be a paved road and a gas street lamp and a church with a steeple. I wish my wife Amanda could be here. But Doc Sawyer says she has to stay close to her room, 'cause I'm gonna be a daddy any day now! (*All cheer. A bugle call is heard offstage.*) Here he comes! Here comes the territorial governor, Longhorn Jim. (*All talk excitedly and gather around the speaker's stand.* TWO CAVALRY TROOPERS, *sabers in belts and bearing bugles, enter, followed by* LONGHORN JIM GARRISON. *He wears a glittering silver and white cowboy vest.*)

1ST TROOPER: At-*ten*-shun! (*All snap to.*)

2ND TROOPER: Presenting His Excellency, the Territorial Governor of Arizona, Mister Longhorn Jim Garrison, himself, in person. (*All cheer.* TROOPERS *play a fanfare, as* GARRISON *ascends speaker's stand.* "*Oh, Promise Me*" *is played on the piano with flourishes and quavers by* CORA LEE, *as* GARRISON *reads from a book.*)

GARRISON: Ahem. (*Reading*) Dearly beloved, we are gathered here at the crossroads of Potluck to join together these folks in a lawful metropolis and an honorable township of public-spirited citizens. Who gives this land unto the town? (THOUSAND-FEATHERS *steps up.*)

THOUSAND-FEATHERS: I give this land for the fair price of fifty dollars cash and a tin bathtub for every one of my hogans.

GARRISON: That's mighty fine. Let us continue. Do you folks promise to love your town, honor its traditions and obey its laws?

ALL (*Together*): We do!

GARRISON: That's mighty fine. And will you build, preserve and defend your town, paying your taxes with a smile?

ALL (*Together*): We will.

GARRISON: And will you raise your children and your grandchildren in this town? (*Stops suddenly. Music stops.*) Hold your mules. Just a bronc-bustin' minute. I can't declare you a town.

ALL (*Ad lib*): What? What did he say? Why not? (*Etc.*)

BOYD: Why not? What's the matter?

GARRISON (*Pointing to book*): Says here — "No area can be considered a true town until it has at least one member of the second generation present." Where's your second generation? (*All look at each other, in dismay. Then, sound of baby crying loudly is heard from off-stage.* DOC SAWYER *enters from hotel, center, with a pink-wrapped bundle in his arms. All cheer.*)

DOC (*Putting baby into* BOYD's *arms*): There you are, Boyd Bluebonnet. Mother and child doing fine! (*Baby's crying is heard again.*)

BOYD: Aww! Isn't she purty? (BY-GOSH *crosses to* BOYD, *taking off his hat respectfully.*)

BY-GOSH: She sure is tiny. (*To baby*) Coochy-coochy-coo. Here, baby, stop that squallin'. Want a little gold nugget, eh?

BOYD (*Crossing down center*): Why, she's not crying. She's singing. Like a lark. That's what I'll call her. Lark. Lark Bluebonnet. First lady of Potluck, Arizona Territory. (*Singing to tune of "Sweet Betsy from Pike"; holding baby proudly*)

Well, I've got me a daughter,

As pink as a rose.

Forget-me-not eyes, and a cute button nose.

I'll work for her, tend her.
Get her home afore dark,
(*Motioning all to join him*)
Come along and say howdy
To my daughter Lark.
(*All cross down to admire baby.*)

ALL (*Singing to tune of "Sweet Betsy from Pike"*):
She's new as the morning, and welcome as Spring,
We'll give her the moon on a long silver string,
She'll grow like a flower, she'll walk like a queen,
The prettiest gal that the West's ever seen!

GARRISON (*Taking off hat to baby*): Well, now, since the second generation has duly arrived, by the authority vested in me, I declare that Potluck is a legally constituted township with all the rights, privileges and paved roads accruing thereto. If anyone knows any reason why Potluck may not become a town, speak now, or — (*Thunderclap is heard.*)

ALL: Ooh . . . ! (*Sound of wind is heard.*)

GRANNY (*Coming forward; with foreboding*): Thunder out of a clear blue sky. (*Sniffing*) Scent of brimstone in the wind. (*Sound of rattles being shaken is heard.*) Rattlesnakes. (*Putting hand to her ear*) He's comin'! He's comin', sure as my name's Granny Conjure! (*Sound of thunder is heard, lights flash, and* BADPENNY, *in black, jumps onstage from down left. All draw back in fright.* GARRISON *jumps from speaker's stand.*)

GARRISON: Badpenny! Scourge of the West. Why do you always turn up to make trouble?

BADPENNY (*Laughing mockingly*): Yes, it's Badpenny. I'm *mortified*. Why, you folks didn't invite me to your ceremony. Here I got myself some brand-new duds, and I waited and waited, and my invitation never came. I'm mighty hurt. I'll have to take a little revenge. (*He lifts his hands. Sound of thunder rolling is heard. All cower in terror.*)

GARRISON: Don't you dare bother these folks, Badpenny. Troopers — run him out of town. (TROOPERS *advance on* BADPENNY.)

BADPENNY: Shazam! (*He waves his hand magically.* TROOPERS *try to pull out sabers, but cannot.*)

1ST TROOPER: My saber's stuck!

2ND TROOPER: So's mine. Why, he's not *human*!

GRANNY: You're right — he's not. He doesn't need a six-shooter. He studied black magic.

ALL (*Ad lib*): Black magic! Oh! (*Etc.*)

BADPENNY: Sure, I've studied black magic. Works a heap better than shootin'. But I need a base of operations. A place like your town. I want to take over Potluck. (*All gasp.* BADPENNY *sings to tune of "Frankie and Johnny."*)

I have a hankerin' for Potluck,
I'd make this town really swing.
Put up saloons and casinos,
Wide open for anything.
I'd be your king, and you could have everything!

GARRISON: King! Why, that is not constitutional!

BADPENNY: Maybe you'd rather I were governor.

GARRISON: Over my dead body.

BADPENNY: That can be arranged. (*He laughs, then slinks over to* GAL SAL. *She turns away. He sings to tune of "Frankie and Johnny"*)

I'd make you the star of my dance halls.
There's room for a sheriff like you —
(*Points to* BOYD, *who shakes his head.*)
If you'd help me rustle some yearlings,

We'd have us a bar-be-cue . . .

(WING DING LEE *hides his eyes.*)

I'd be your king, and you could have everything.

Let me be king, and you can do anything!

ALL (*Advancing on* BADPENNY; *ad lib*): Out! Get out, Badpenny! Vamoose! Don't come back! (*Etc. Sound of rattles is heard.*)

BADPENNY (*Enraged*): Fools! I'll make you suffer for that. (*Spying baby in* BOYD's *arms*) What's this? (BOYD *steps back, covering baby protectively.*) A sweet baby girl.

BOYD: Don't you come near her, Badpenny.

BADPENNY: What'll you do? Shoot me? Bullets can't touch me. But with just a blink of my eye I can turn that sweet baby girl into an ugly old horned toad!

ALL (*Together*): No!

BADPENNY: Tell you what I'm going to do. I won't change her into a toad. I'll bide my time until you get to know her and love her. Then, on her sixteenth birthday, she'll prick her finger on a piece of barbed wire, and she'll fall down (*As sound of rattles is heard*) . . . dead! (*As thunder rolls, and lights flash,* BADPENNY *exits, laughing.*)

ALL (*Together*): No, no, no!

CORA LEE: Form a committee. Outlaw barbed wire!

GARRISON: I'll call out the Cavalry and scour the country for barbed wire.

BY-GOSH: Ship it out of town, by gosh!

BOYD (*Addressing baby in his arms*): Don't you worry, honey. I'll see to it that by the time you're sixteen, there won't be a scrap of barbed wire in all of Arizona Territory. (GRANNY *shakes her head sadly, crossing down center.*)

GRANNY: Won't do a mite of good against Badpenny. You've got to have a stronger spell than his.

BOYD: Granny, you're a witch-woman. You know about spells, don't you? You can out-spell him, can't you?

GRANNY (*Sighing*): No, Boyd Bluebonnet. He's stronger and smarter than I am. It'd take a heap of studying to undo Badpenny's spell.

BOYD: Will you study up, Granny?

ALL: (*Together*): Please, Granny!

GRANNY: I'll try. I'll study spells morning, noon and night. But we only have sixteen years to find the answer.

BOYD: Sixteen years.

GRANNY (*As curtain closes*): And those years will fly by so fast you'll think they were the short week in February. . . . (*Curtain, followed by an interlude of Western tunes while the scene is changed.*)

* * * * *

SCENE 2

TIME: *Sixteen years later; Lark's sixteenth birthday, in the evening.*

SETTING: *Same as Scene 1, with speaker's stand removed. A bank and a church have been added right and left of other buildings, and there is a gas street lamp already lit, up center next to hotel. Japanese lanterns are strung along hotel balustrade. At left center are barbecue table and benches. Table is decked for a party, with white tablecloth, bowls of lilacs, gifts, and pink streamers. Piano, decked with streamers, is at left.*

AT RISE: CORA LEE *sits at piano.* GRANNY *sits in a rocker on the hotel porch, a huge pile of dusty books beside her. She reads swiftly and silently, her spectacles on her nose, and her lips moving as she pores over the books.*

BY-GOSH, DOC, BOYD, AMANDA BLUEBONNET, *and* GAL SAL, *with* TOWNSPEOPLE, *are gathered onstage.* CHIEF THOUSAND-FEATHERS *stands up center, by hotel door, his arms folded.* WING DING LEE *holds a huge, tiered birthday cake with candles. All look prosperous in fashionable Western finery.*

ALL (*Singing to tune of "There'll Be a Hot Time in the Old Town Tonight"; confidentially to audience*):
Big round moon, above the mountain crest,
Tinklin' tunes, the town in Sunday best,
Wink your eyes, and keep it a surprise —
There'll be a *birthday* in Potluck tonight!

GAL SAL (*Singing*):
Don't you tell —

AMANDA (*Singing*):
Not a tattle, not a tip!

CORA LEE (*Singing*):
Mum's the word —

BY-GOSH (*Singing*):
Button up your lip!

DOC (*Singing*):
Cat's in the bag. Don't let the secret slip —

ALL (*Singing*):
There'll be a *birthday* in Potluck tonight,
A sixteenth birthday in Potluck tonight! Shh!

(FOUR COWBOYS, *carrying nosegays, enter up right.*)

1ST COWBOY (*Loudly*): Hey, where's the birthday girl? Where's our Miss Lark? Where is she, Mrs. Bluebonnet?

OTHERS: Shh!

AMANDA: Hush up now, you boys. Lark doesn't know a blessed thing about this party. She thinks she's going to a church meeting. (*To* BOYD) Ready, Pa? Everybody hide behind the table. (*All scurry behind table.* BOYD *crosses to street lamp, taking a douser on a pole from hotel porch to quench lamp.*) Lights out, Pa! (BOYD *quenches lamp. Lights dim.*)

BOYD (*Calling into hotel*): Lark? Come on, honey. Time for the church meeting. (*All giggle.*)

LARK (*From inside hotel*): I'm coming, Pa. (*All giggle again. Spotlight catches* LARK *as she enters through hotel door. She wears a gauzy white dress with a blue sash and her long hair is tied back with a ribbon.*) Pa? What's the matter with the lamp? I can't see my hand in front of my face.

BOYD: Reckon the wind blew it out, honey.

LARK (*Sighing*): You know, it's a funny thing. Here I am sixteen years old today, and nobody wished me a happy birthday. (*All smother giggles.*) What was that?

BOYD: Field mice chatterin', I reckon.

LARK: You know, Pa, it would have been nice to have a cake. Just a small cake. Even a cupcake. (BOYD *lights lamp with the other side of the douser. Lights come up full.* LARK *blinks, and rubs her eyes, astonished*)

ALL (*Jumping up*): Surprise!

COWBOYS (*Presenting nosegays*): Happy birthday, Miss Lark.

LARK (*Accepting nosegays*): Oh! You remembered my birthday. Why, you sweet old things! (*She kisses each* COWBOY *impulsively.*)

COWBOYS: Wahoo! (*They do somersaults and backflips.*)

1ST COWBOY: She branded me!

2ND COWBOY: I'm gonna faint with dee-light!

3RD COWBOY: I'll never wash my face again. No, siree!

4TH COWBOY: Gol-ly. She went and did what no gal ever did before. She kissed me!

COWBOYS: Wahoo!

BOYD (*Clapping hands for order*): Ladies and gents and cowboys. Grab your partners for a happy birthday dance in honor of Miss Lark Bluebonnet! (*All cheer and all except* GRANNY, CORA LEE *and* CHIEF THOUSAND-FEATHERS *dance a lively reel, to live or recorded music, cheering and waving their hats and handkerchiefs at the conclusion.* WING DING LEE *puts cake on table.*)

AMANDA (*Motioning everybody to table*): Folks, come gather around for the gift-givin' and chow-eatin' and general celebratin' till dawn. (*All crowd around table.*)

ALL (*Ad lib*): Open my gift, Lark! Mine first! (*Etc.* LARK *takes place of honor at head of table, opens gifts excitedly.*)

LARK: Heavens to Betsy, there are enough presents here for the Queen of Sheba. (*She holds up each gift admiringly.*) Oh, look — a *gold nugget.* And a scroll deeding me a lake and a pine forest and a wigwam. Thanks, Chief Thousand-Feathers. I always wanted my own wigwam. (*Holding up shoes*) Look at these — silver dancing slippers from Gal Sal. And piano lessons in a book from Miss Cora Lee Hoopwell. And this cake — this beautiful cake! It's too much. I'm so happy being sixteen, I'm not sure I want to be seventeen! (*Singing to tune of "Beautiful Dreamer"*)

> Beautiful birthday, day of my dreams,
> Lilacs and lanterns and silver moonbeams.
> Dancing and laughter, friends everywhere,
> Cake on the table and songs in the air.
> How can I thank you? What can I say?
> Bless you for one perfect rose of a day!
> I'll always remember your sweet, secret schemes —
> Beautiful birthday, the day of my dreams.

Beautiful birthday, the day of my dreams . . .
(*All applaud at song's end.*)

BY-GOSH: Say — you know what? We've done it!

AMANDA: Done what?

BY-GOSH: Well, here it is, after sundown, on Miss Lark's sixteenth birthday, and nary a thing's happened to her. We've beaten him. We've beaten old Badpenny!

OTHERS: Hooray! We've beaten Badpenny.

GRANNY (*Rising and shaking head warningly*): The day's not over yet. (*Sound of hoofbeats rapidly approaching is heard.* BADPENNY, *disguised as a Pony Express rider, hat pulled down on face, runs in, bearing a gaily wrapped gift.* LARK *runs to meet him.*)

BADPENNY: Special Delivery for Miss Lark Bluebonnet of Potluck. A birthday present from Governor Longhorn Jim Garrison.

GRANNY (*Suspiciously*): Wait, Lark! Don't be so hasty!

LARK (*Opening gift*): A present from the governor himself. Glory be! There's no end to my birthday. (*Sound of rattles is heard from offstage.*) How strange . . . How very strange! (LARK *holds up a piece of barbed wire.*)

BOYD (*Shocked*): Barbed wire!

GRANNY: Drop it, Lark! Drop it as you would a rattlesnake! (LARK *drops wire, crying out as she does so.*)

LARK: It's pricked me. I'm bleeding. (*Sound of rattles is heard.*)

BADPENNY (*Pushing his hat back, and laughing mockingly*): Happy birthday, Miss Lark. You got your wish. Now you'll be sixteen . . . forever.

ALL: Badpenny! (BOYD, AMANDA *and* DOC *run down to* LARK, *as she totters, sways and falls into* BOYD's *arms.* BOYD *kneels, cradling her head in his arms.*)

Doc (*Kneeling, and taking her hand*): Her pulse is failing. She's dying!

AMANDA: No, no. (*Lifting her arms in supplication to* BADPENNY) We'll do anything. We'll give you every-thing. Bring her back. Oh, please. Bring her back to life!

BADPENNY: Too late. She'll die, and when she breathes her last, the town will die, too. (*He waves his hand magically.*) Bring on the barbed wire! (BARBED WIRE GANG, *in black, with black masks, enter. They bring on rolls of barbed wire — coils of rope with stiff paper barbs, painted silver. Others, except* GRANNY, *freeze in place.*)

BARBED WIRE GANG (*Singing to tune of "When Johnny Comes Marching Home Again"*):
Around and around the town we go,
Barbed wire, barbed wire.
Fencing you in from head to toe,
Barbed wire, barbed wire.
Sharp as the fang of a rattlesnake,
The wire will stab and scratch and rake,
And you'll ne'er get free of
A prison of twisted wire!

1ST GANG MEMBER (*Singing*):
It'll keep you put for a thousand years.

GANG (*Singing*):
Barbed wire. Barbed wire.

2ND GANG MEMBER (*Singing*):
Though you rust the fence with a million tears.

GANG (*Singing*):
Barbed wire. Barbed wire.

3RD GANG MEMBER (*Singing*):
Though you clip and cut with snips for tin,

4TH GANG MEMBER (*Singing*):
> You cannot tunnel a loophole in,

GANG (*Singing*):
> And you'll rot forever —
> Behind a corral of wire,
> (*Repeat phrase*) A picket of twisted wire,
> A thicket of winding wire,
> (*Shouting*) Barbed wire!

BADPENNY (*Laughing exultantly*): Nothing's stronger than barbed wire.

GRANNY (*Crossing center*): Badpenny, all these years I've been studying. I can't undo your spell, but I can gentle it down, and I can put Miss Lark and Potluck out of your reach forever. (*She turns to others, who are frozen in place. "Sweet Betsy from Pike" is played slowly and softly behind* GRANNY's *speech.*) Snooze, drowse, dream. Close your eyes and sink into a trance. (*All close eyes, heads nodding.* BY-GOSH *snores.*) Nod and nap for a hundred years, long after wicked Badpenny has wrinkled up and fallen to dust. Listen! I'm sending a song into the air. A song to fetch Lark's own true love wherever he may be in space and time. When he hears the song, he'll come to her and wake her with a kiss. And Potluck will yawn and stretch and come alive again . . . (*Singing to "Sweet Betsy from Pike"*)
> Oh, hear while I tell of the girl they call Lark,
> All spellbound in slumber through years long and
> dark.
> Oh, find her and wake her, and wed her right soon,
> E'er she sleep on forever beneath the cold moon . . .

(BARBED WIRE GANG *begins to stretch out the coils of rope across stage. Rattles are heard and* BADPENNY

laughs mockingly. As wire conceals GRANNY, *she yawns, singing reprise of the last line, softly.*)
　　E'er she sleep on . . . forever . . . beneath the cold moon.
(*Curtain*)

* * * * *

SCENE 3

TIME: *A hundred years later.*

BEFORE RISE: *A sign, reading* BUS DEPOT, BARRIER, ARIZONA *is in front of curtain.* JOHNNY THOUSAND-FEATHERS, *in jeans and fringed jacket and wearing an Indian headband, enters with guitar slung over his back, carrying a basket of Indian pottery, jewelry and blankets, which he sets out on stage. He sits cross-legged beside his wares. Bus horn toots offstage, and sound of bus motor drawing up to bus stop is heard.*

OFFSTAGE VOICE: All out for Barrier, Arizona. Rest stop for five minutes. (TOM LAWRENCE, *in hiking clothes, wearing backpack, enters left. He crosses to* JOHNNY, *who holds up a necklace.*)

JOHNNY: Hey, pal. Want to buy a genuine turquoise necklace for your sweetie? (TOM *takes off backpack.*)

TOM (*Examining necklace and handing it back*): I don't have a sweetie, pal. And if I did I wouldn't buy her a necklace made by a Japanese Indian from Yokohama.

JOHNNY: Are you calling me a fake? I'm Johnny Thousand-Feathers, a direct descendant of Chief Thousand-Feathers, who disappeared from the face of the earth one hundred years ago to the day.

TOM: Oh, sure. And I'm George Washington's nephew.

JOHNNY: Come on, pal. How about a blanket? A nice vase for your mother?

TOM: Not interested. Neither is my mother.

JOHNNY: Listen, I'm a licensed guide. How about visiting the historic barbed-wire barrier? Man, it's more historic than the Alamo. Miles of rusty barbed wire, a hundred years old. Some say there's a ghost town inside it.

TOM: Ruins put me to sleep. The only guide I'll need is to the local folklore society. I'm a folk-song specialist on a fellowship to research Western folk songs.

JOHNNY (*Brightly*): Folk songs? You've come to the right man. How about twenty verses of "Home on the Range" for a buck and a half? (TOM *shakes his head*.) "The Streets of Laredo" for fifty cents? (TOM *grimaces and starts to walk off right*) Listen! (*He swings his guitar around and sings to tune of "Sweet Betsy from Pike"*)

Oh, hear while I tell of the girl they call Lark . . .

(TOM *turns, interested, and* JOHNNY *sings on with great expression.*)

All spellbound in slumber through years long and dark,
Oh, find her and wake her and wed her right soon,
E'er she sleep on forever beneath the cold moon.

TOM (*Singing last line*):

E'er she sleep on forever beneath the cold moon.

(*Pauses*) Strange. I know the tune — "Sweet Betsy from Pike." But the words are different. Haunting. Who was this Lark, anyhow? Where did she live? What did she look like?

JOHNNY (*Bargaining*): You want to know about Lark? I'll tell you all I know about her if you let me take you to the barbed-wire barrier. Five dollars. That's my rock-bottom price, and I'll throw in the story for free.

TOM: It's a deal. Lead on, Johnny Thousand-Feathers!

(JOHNNY *packs up his wares.* TOM *takes backpack and*

JOHNNY *slings guitar across his back as they exit down right. Sign is removed and curtains open.*)

*　*　*

SETTING: *The same as at end of Scene 2, with barrier of rusty barbed wire stretched across stage. Barrier is made of coils of wire attached to two flats painted to look like thick, impenetrable fence. Hats of various historical periods are caught here and there in the barrier.*

AT RISE: *Characters from Scene 2 are in place, out of sight, behind barrier.* JOHNNY *enters, followed by* TOM. *They remove backpack and guitar and inspect barrier.*

JOHNNY: There it is: the mysterious barbed-wire barrier. Nobody knows what it is, or why it is, or how to get through it. They've tried tanks and dynamite and flame throwers. Those hats you see (*Pointing*) — they're all that's left of fellows who've tried to get through on their own. There's a Rough Rider's hat, and a Mexican sombrero, and a World War One helmet. There's even a top hat from some dude who came out West with a pair of white gloves and a silver shovel to try to tunnel under the barrier. They'd all heard Lark's song, you see — and it got to them just as it got to you — er, what did you say your name was?

TOM: Tom Lawrence. You know, I've always had this *thing* about folk songs. I've always wanted to discover the rarest, most beautiful song — the ultimate song. And now I've found it, and it isn't enough. I have to go on and find the girl behind it — Lark.

JOHNNY: Lark? Come on, man. She's a legend. A spooky legend. Hey — it's getting late. I don't want to stay out here after sunset. Funny things go on around here when it gets dark.

Tom: Go ahead. I'll come back on my own. (*He paces beside barrier.*) There must be a way to get through this barrier.

Johnny: Oh, no! Not another barrier freak. Listen, Tom, take my advice. Turn around and point yourself toward town before it's too late. They say men have vanished in there. They say there are human skeletons in there. (Tom *ignores him, and begins to try to part the wire. As he does so, sound of rattles is heard.*)

Tom: Maybe if I twisted this section, *here* — (*Sound of thunder is heard, lights flash, and wire parts, pulled slowly offstage.* Johnny *rubs his eyes in disbelief, and* Tom *gapes as characters in Potluck are revealed, frozen in sleep as in Scene 2.*)

Johnny: What did you do? The barbed wire just — just *melted.*

Tom: I don't know! One minute the barrier was there and the next it wasn't. Look! (*They cross upstage, examining the figures of* Boyd, Amanda, By-Gosh, Doc, Granny, Wing Ding, Cora Lee, *and* Townspeople. Johnny *gingerly pokes* Chief Thousand-Feathers.)

Johnny (*Awed*): Who are they, Tom? Do you think maybe they're waxworks? (By-Gosh *snores.*)

Tom (*Startled*): Did you hear that? The old-timer's snoring. I never heard of waxworks snoring. (Johnny *crosses to cake, taking a scoop of frosting on his finger and licking it, while* Tom *crosses to* Lark.)

Johnny: The cake's still fresh. (*He gazes around, baffled*) Say — do you think we've wandered onto a movie set?

Tom: This is no movie, Johnny. These people are all asleep! (*He slaps* Lark*'s hand gently.*) Hey, wake up. (*He looks at her closely.*) Johnny! Do you know who this is? It's Lark! I've found Lark!

Johnny: Then this is the lost town of Potluck. (*Crossing

to CHIEF THOUSAND-FEATHERS) And this must be Chief
Thousand-Feathers, my great-great grandfather. (*He
shakes* CHIEF THOUSAND-FEATHERS, *who does not re-
spond.*) Wake up, Grandpa! (*Yelling at the top of his
lungs*) Wake up, everybody!

TOM (*Shaking his head*): Save your breath. What does
the song say? They're all "spellbound in slumber."

JOHNNY: Spellbound? You mean we have to mumble a lot
of mumbo-jumbo and draw pentagrams on the ground?
Well — go on. You're the folklore specialist. Don't you
know about spells?

TOM: Not much. My major was ethnic music. Listen,
you're an Indian. Doesn't magic come naturally to you?

JOHNNY: Not to me, pal. My major was accounting. Can't
you think of *anything?*

TOM: Well . . . (*Embarrassed*) In the old legends there
was one sure way to wake a sleeping maiden. The only
thing is — we haven't been introduced.

JOHNNY: What do you mean, you haven't been introduced?

TOM: Well, this involves — it consists of — *kissing* her.

JOHNNY: Kissing her? Well, go on and do it. My grandpa's about to fall on his head and fracture his feathers.
(*As* TOM *hesitates,* JOHNNY *crosses to him.*) If you don't
kiss her, *I* will. (TOM *kisses* LARK. *"Sweet Betsy from
Pike" is heard. All onstage yawn and stretch, in place.*
LARK *stirs and sits up, blinking at* TOM, *who pulls her
up beside him.*)

TOM: Ahem. Er — how do you do. My name is Tom
Lawrence, and I'd like to explain about that kiss.

LARK: How do you do, Tom Lawrence? I'm Lark Bluebonnet, and it's my opinion that a kiss is somethin' that
nobody ever needs to explain. (*She yawns.*) It was

mighty sweet of you to waken me that way. Sure beats cold water on the face!

BOYD (*Yawning, puzzled*): Now what was I saying, just before I nodded off? (*He rises.*)

DOC: I had such a funny dream (*Rising to his feet*) about a sidewinder named Badpenny.

GRANNY (*Shaking sleep off*): Badpenny! (*She rises from rocker, and runs right.*) I have to find out what happened to that varmint! (*Exits*)

AMANDA: I can't think what came over me. I seem to have dozed off for a minute. Folks — folks — let's go right on with Miss Lark's sixteenth birthday. How about a square dance?

ALL: Hooray! (*All take places for square dance as "There'll Be a Hot Time in the Old Town Tonight" is played softly behind dialogue.*)

JOHNNY (*Pulling* TOM, *who leaves* LARK *reluctantly*): Come here, Tom. We have a problem.

TOM (*Looking back at* LARK): Don't go away, Lark, I have the first dance.

LARK: Don't you fret, Tom Lawrence. I've got my whole dance program open for you!

BOYD: Grab your partners for the Grand Promenade. (*Music continues to play behind the dialogue.* GRANNY *runs onstage, holding up a skeleton with* BADPENNY's *hat and scarf on it. As she shakes it, sound of soft rattling is heard.*)

GRANNY: Look, everybody. Look who I found. It's Badpenny. He was caught in his own barbed wire. He'll make a mighty good scarecrow for my herb garden. (*All laugh.* JOHNNY *pulls* TOM *downstage. All others clap softly, standing in place as music continues.*)

JOHNNY: Tom — they don't know it's the twentieth

century! They think it's a hundred years ago. They don't know about automobiles, or television, or landing on the moon.

TOM: Right. And they don't know about pollution, or missiles, or overpopulation, either.

JOHNNY: What a story! I can see the headlines. "Town sleeps for a hundred years." We should tell the whole world about them.

TOM (*Shaking his head*): Not yet. If we're not very careful, the wrong people will get hold of Potluck and turn it into a zoo. You wouldn't want that, would you?

JOHNNY: Of course not. But we can't leave them like this, Tom. My grandpa would die of fright if an automobile came down Main Street.

TOM: We'll stay and break the news a little at a time. We'll show them the world with all its technology and its problems.

JOHNNY: Yeah. Let them get to know the modern world before it gets to know them.

TOM: They had an up-and-coming town. They may want paved roads and parking meters. But maybe they won't like what they see. Maybe they'll want to take another path. They ought to have a choice. Is it a deal? (*Extending his hand*)

JOHNNY (*Grasping his hand warmly*): It's a deal! (LARK *runs downstage, taking* TOM *by the hand and drawing him into square dance.*)

LARK: Come on, Tom Lawrence. It's dancin' time for you and me. (*Music continues. Sound of a jet plane is heard from offstage. All look up.*)

CHIEF THOUSAND-FEATHERS (*Pointing up excitedly*): An eagle with fire in its tail. A good omen for Potluck!

JOHNNY (*Amused*): How about that? Grandpa saw his first jet plane!

ALL (*Singing to tune of "There'll Be a Hot Time in the Old Town Tonight"*):

    When you see an eagle in the sky,

    There will be rejoicing by and by,

    The stage will roll, and wagon wheels will hum,

    And there'll be good times in Potluck to come!

GAL SAL (*Singing*):

    Full hotels —

BY-GOSH (*Singing*):

    And gold dust everywhere —

AMANDA (*Singing*):

    Wedding bells —

LARK (*Singing*):

    And rainbows in the air —

WING DING (*Singing*):

    Egg foo yung —

CORA LEE (*Singing*):

    Pianny tunes to strum —

ALL (*Singing*):

    And there'll be good times in Potluck to come!

    Glory hallelujah! Good times in Potluck to come!

    (*All square dance to "There'll Be a Hot Time in the Old Town Tonight." At conclusion,* LARK *kisses* TOM.)

LARK: There! I paid you back proper for wakin' me up!

ALL (*Singing*):

    And there'll be good times in Potluck to come!

(*Curtain*)

THE END

The Town That Couldn't Wake Up

PRODUCTION NOTES

Characters: 19 male; 5 female; male offstage voice; as many male and female as desired for Townspeople.

Playing Time: 35 minutes.

Costumes: Western dress. Women wear long dresses and shawls; men wear plaid shirts, jeans, wide-brimmed hats. If desired, they may wear fancier dress for Scene 2. Chief Thousand-Feathers wears Indian outfit; Wing Ding Lee, white apron, chef's hat. Granny has spectacles, white wig. Longhorn Jim wears silver cowboy vest. Badpenny is dressed in black, as are outlaws, who also wear masks. He later wears Pony Express rider's outfit. Cavalry troopers wear uniforms with sabers. Lark wears white party dress with blue sash. Johnny wears jeans and fringed jacket and headband. Tom wears hiking outfit.

Properties: Plate of spareribs; scroll; books; doll wrapped in pink blanket; birthday cake; four nosegays; douser; wrapped gifts containing shoes, scroll, music, gold nugget, and piece of barbed wire; coils of rope with silver barbs for barbed wire barrier; guitar; basket of Indian jewelry, pottery and blankets; backpack; skeleton with black hat and scarf.

Setting: Scene 1: The frontier town of Potluck, Arizona Territory. Hotel with swinging doors is at center, with balustrade. Rocking chair is on porch. Stores are on either side of hotel, with signs as indicated in text. Speaker's stand hung with bunting is right center with piano beside it. Scene 2: Same as Scene 1, except that bank and church are right and left of other buildings. There is a gas street lamp next to hotel. Barbecue table with white tablecloth, bowls of lilacs, wrapped birthday gifts and pink streamers is left center with piano, also decked with streamers, beside it. Speaker's stand has been removed. Scene 3: Barrier of rusty barbed wire (two flats that can be drawn offstage) with hats from different historical periods hides the town, which is the same as in Scene 2. For the Before Rise, a sign reading: BUS DEPOT, BARRIER, ARIZONA, is in front of curtain.

Lighting: Flashes of light when Badpenny enters and exits; dimming of lights when street lamp is extinguished, as indicated in text.

Sound: Offstage thunder, wind, rattling noise, bus horn, jet plane, as indicated in text. Live piano music, performed by actor playing Cora Lee, accompanies songs, or recorded music may be played offstage while piano playing is pantomimed.

THE FASTEST THIMBLE IN THE WEST

The Fastest Thimble in the West

A new look at "The Brave Little Tailor"

Characters

MA COZY, *Superintendent of Ma Cozy's Home for Happy Orphans*
TWO-BITS, *an older girl orphan*
HENRY, *an older boy orphan*
OLIVER
NICHOLAS
DAVEY
ANNIE } *other orphans*
EM
NELL
LAWYER GRUDGE, *meanest man in the East*
ANONYMOUS JONES, *one who is not what he seems*
WELLS FARGO MAN
BRUTE MCGURK, *meanest man in the West*
LOATHSOME TOAD } *McGurk's evil sidekicks*
ONE-EYED JACK
FOUR COWBOYS
TOWNSPEOPLE, *6 men and 6 women*
FOUR DELSARTE DANCERS
BARD KEEPER

SCENE 1

TIME: *Way back when — a stormy evening when anything might happen.*

SETTING: *Parlor of Ma Cozy's Home for Happy Orphans.*

AT RISE: TWO-BITS *and* HENRY *are sitting in wing chairs, on either side of fireplace, up left.* ANNIE, EM *and* NELL *cluster around* TWO-BITS, *who is winding* ANNIE'*s hair in rag curls.* OLIVER, NICHOLAS *and* DAVEY *sit crosslegged on floor around* HENRY. *He is sitting crosslegged in chair, stitching buttonhole on frock coat worn by tailor's dummy in front of him. Top hat adorns dummy. Sound of wind whistling is heard.*

TWO-BITS: Listen to that wind! Do you know who's out in that storm?

EM: Poor little orphans like us, with no mamas and no papas and no nice warm home. (*Shivering*) Brr-r!

OTHERS (*Shivering*): Brr-r!

HENRY: If it weren't for Ma Cozy, we'd be out there shivering too. But Ma Cozy, bless her heart, took us all in and gave us a *home.*

ALL (*Singing and clapping to tune of "Skip to My Lou"*):
    Home, home, we've got a home,
    Home, home, we've got a home,
    Home, home, we've got a home,
    Home, sweet home, Ma Cozy!
(ANNIE *and* NICHOLAS *sashay downstage and do pat-a-cake in rhythm to music.*)

ANNIE (*Singing*):
    Happy little orphans, perky as you please,
    Running in the meadows, playing in the trees,

NICHOLAS (*Singing*):
    Don't need a mom, Ma Cozy'll do,
    I'll take Ma Cozy for a papa too!
(*They sashay back to place.*)

ALL (*Singing and clapping*):
    Home, home, we've got a home,
    Home, home, we've got a home,
    Home, home, we've got a home,
    Home, sweet home, Ma Cozy!
    (MA COZY *enters with tea cart containing tray with mugs, pitcher of cocoa, and bowl of marshmallows.*)

MA COZY: Cocoa time, children! (*All cheer.* TWO-BITS *and* HENRY *help* MA COZY *pass around cocoa.* OLIVER *gulps down cocoa, holds out mug.*)

OLIVER: Please, Ma Cozy. May I have more?

MA COZY: Why, of course, Oliver. One marshmallow — or two?

OLIVER: Two, please. (MA COZY *puts two marshmallows into his mug.*)

TWO-BITS: Cocoa with marshmallows! Why, we're the only institution in the state with overfed orphans. (*Knock at door is heard.*)

NELL (*Running to door*): I'll bet it's a little stranger! Somebody always leaves a baby on our doorstep when it's stormy. (*She opens door. Snow is thrown in, and sound of rising wind is heard.* NELL *pulls in a washbasket.*)

ANNIE: Tell us, Nell. What is it this time? Pink or blue?

NELL (*Holding up basket*): Pink. (*Girls cheer.* HENRY *begins sewing again.*)

TWO-BITS: Another basket baby. We've got half a dozen already. Where'll I put her, Ma Cozy?

MA COZY: Pull out the bottom drawer of my chifforobe. I think there's one drawer left. Remember, there's always room for one more. (TWO-BITS, *sighing and shaking head, exits up left with basket. She re-enters during* HENRY*'s speech.*)

HENRY (*Snipping thread with flourish*): There. It's done,

Oliver. Your Sunday-go-to-meeting coat is finished. (*He brushes coat.*) When you wear this coat, you mind your manners, Oliver. Clothes make the man, that's my theory. Why — the course of history itself might have been changed by the right tailoring. You take Julius Caesar, for example. (*"Talking blues" music begins playing improvised tune or vamp under* HENRY's *lines.*)

> Now, if Caesar's royal toga had a pleated drape,
> And his tunic had been cut and pinned to fit his shape,
> He'd have stayed at home in downtown Rome to strut and pose,
> And Gaul would be *united* by the Emperor's new clothes!

ALL (*Chanting*):

> More, more, tell us more.
> Henry, keep a-talking and tell us more.

HENRY:

> Mr. Benedict Arnold was another famous gent,
> Who might have made the winning team wherever he went,
> But his favorite haberdasher dashed into the woods and quit,
> So Ben bolted to the British 'cause his britches didn't fit!

ALL (*Chanting*):

> More, more, tell us more.
> Henry, keep a-talking and tell us more.

HENRY:

> Well, you know how old Napoleon stood, his sword hand in his vest?
> Why, he could hardly fight at all for clutching at his chest.

If they'd sewed his buttons tighter on his shirtwaist,
    it is true —
He'd have drowned the opposition down at —
    Waterloo!

(*Music vamps into "Oh, Dem Golden Slippers." All clap.* OLIVER *dons new coat and top hat. Using fire poker as a cane, he struts downstage.*)

ALL (*Singing to tune of "Oh, Dem Golden Slippers"*):
    Throw away those sad rags,
    Go, display your glad rags,
    There's a wise old platitude,
    "It's the duds that make the dude —"
    Keep your tailor handy,
    You'll look fine and dandy,
    Promenadin' new and neat,
    To give the world a treat!

(*Music continues with reprise of song as* OLIVER *performs cakewalk, finishing to applause, and bowing. Thundering knock at door is heard.*)

MA COZY: Another dear little stranger! I'll close my eyes, children, and you surprise me. (*She puts hands over eyes.* TWO-BITS *opens door wide. Dramatic sting chord is played. Snow is thrown onstage, and sound of wind rising is heard.* LAWYER GRUDGE *leaps in, twirling moustache.*) Pink or blue? Boy or girl?

ALL (*Together*): The meanest man in the East!

TWO-BITS: Lawyer Grudge!

MA COZY (*Uncovering eyes; warily*): What do you want with us, Lawyer Grudge? I know you only come to bring bad news to those who have lost their wherewithal.

GRUDGE: True, madam. It gives me great pleasure to announce that your wherewithal has dribbled away to *nothing*. In short, I am about to foreclose your mortgage, madam, and turn you and these orphans out into the cold. (*Orphans wail.*)

EM: Lawyer Grudge, what makes you so mean to little children? (*"Man on the Flying Trapeze" is played softly in background.*)

GRUDGE (*Singing to "Man on the Flying Trapeze"*):
Once I had hopes for a nephew of mine —
To tread in my footsteps, at banking to shine.
A human abacus, his math was divine!
'Til the circus appeared in our town.

Now my nephew fell hard for a rider,
She wore bangles and spangles and beads,
And the night we were having an audit,
He vanished with all of my dee-eds!

(*Chorus*)
He rode out of town with the circus that night,
But a twister, alas, struck him down in his flight,
Yet they tell me a small Grudge survives him somewhere —
To my fortune that child is the heir!

(*Speaking*) Yes, my nephew Ralph has a child somewhere in the world. Until that child is found, I will wreak vengeance upon all children. Out! Out you miserable moppets! (*He flings door open. Sound of wind rising is heard, and snow is thrown onstage.*)

ANNIE (*On her knees, pleading*): Into the snow, sir?

OTHERS (*On their knees*): Oh, no, sir!

HENRY (*Slamming door shut, standing guard*): Stop! (*Fanfare is played.*) I will save this happy home! (*All cheer and clap.*) Mr. Grudge, before this month is up, I will restore the fortunes of the orphanage!

GRUDGE: You? A penniless pauper without a proper papa? How will you make your fortune?

HENRY: How? Why — I'll go out West! Think of it — thousands of acres of land . . . Mountains sparkling with silver and gold . . . And for my skill as a tailor, cash. Cash on the barrelhead. (*Dramatic chord is played on piano.*)

GRUDGE: Cash! You said the magic word. (*Handing* HENRY *document and pen*) Sign here, before I change my mind. (HENRY *signs boldly.*) You have just agreed to pay me five thousand dollars before the month is up. If you cannot pay up, you become my miserable servant, doomed to add, subtract and foreclose for the rest of your natural life. (*Crossing to door*) Farewell. I shall return on the stroke of the passing of the old month. Have the cash in tidy bundles, or —

ALL (*Fearfully*): Or?

GRUDGE: Into the cold, cruel world with you — all of you! (*Laughing wickedly, he twirls moustache, flings cape about him, and exits. Orphans boo. Music to "Seeing Nellie Home" is played.* HENRY *dons coat and slings bundle over his shoulder.* TWO-BITS *does the same.*)

HENRY (*Singing to tune of "Seeing Nellie Home"*):
　　Here's my coat, and here's my bundle,
　　I'll doff my hat and wave goodbye (*Tips cap*),
　　For it's westward ho, and off I go-o,
　　To give the West a try.

(*To* TWO-BITS) Say, Two-Bits, where do you think you're going?

TWO-BITS: With you, Henry. With you. (*Sings to tune of "Seeing Nellie Home"*)

You need someone rough and ready,
With two fists and grit that's true.
You need someone brave when the going's grave,
So I'm coming West with you!

ALL (*Singing to tune of "Seeing Nellie Home"*):
You are saving our Cozy home,
Saving our Cozy home,
How can we repay what you're doing today,
Saving our Cozy home?

MA COZY (*Bringing sewing basket to* TWO-BITS *and* HENRY): My dear noble children! Before you depart, let me give you some keepsakes. Two-Bits, sixteen years ago you were left in a basket on our doorstep. (*Plucks out a piece of torn parchment*) This bit of paper was pinned to your raggedy pink blanket. It has a coat of arms on it with cash boxes rampant on a field of gold coins. That's why we nicknamed you "Two-Bits." Find the other half of this paper and you will solve the mystery of your parentage.

TWO-BITS (*Pocketing parchment*): Thank you, Ma Cozy. I'll keep it close always. (*"Seeing Nellie Home" is played softly in background.*)

MA COZY: Now, Henry. Stand straight and tall. (*Draping a measuring tape around his neck*) Let this measuring tape remind you to measure up to your true self. (*Putting a bandolier of threads around his shoulders*) May these threads tie you to your loved ones here. (*Fastening scissors in a holster around his waist*) Use these scissors to cut the cloth fair and true. And now, Henry, put out your finger.

HENRY: Oh, no, Ma Cozy. Not that! I couldn't take your sterling silver thimble. Not the thimble Captain Cozy gave you afore he was lost at sea.

MA COZY: Please, Henry. I want you to have it. (*She slips thimble onto his finger*) You'll be going West, where there are many temptations for a fine young man. Henry, promise me you won't lie, or cuss, or drink distilled spirits. And above all, promise me on this silver thimble that you will never shoot a gun!

HENRY (*Raising his hand*): I solemnly promise. (OLIVER *dashes up to umbrella stand, takes out gaudily decorated flyswatter and gives it to* HENRY.)

OLIVER: I was going to save this for your birthday, but here 'tis. A real, homemade flyswatter.

HENRY: Why, thanks a heap, Oliver. (*Sniffs loudly*) We'd best go, Two-Bits, before I start bawling.

TWO-BITS: Goodbye, everybody. And don't worry a speck. You can bet your bottom dollar we'll be back afore the money's due. (*They exit.* MA COZY *and orphans cross to window, waving.*)

MA COZY (*Lighting candle*): I'll light this candle for them until they return. Perhaps it will light my dear husband's return, too. For I have such a strong feeling, here in my heart, that he too will come back to us someday. (*"Seeing Nellie Home" is played.*)

ALL (*Singing softly to "Seeing Nellie Home"*):
You are saving our Cozy home,
Saving our Cozy home.
How can we repay you, Two-Bits and Henry,
For saving our Cozy home?

(*All remain in tableau at window as curtains slowly close. Medley of Western music is played as scene is changed.*)

*   *   *   *   *

SCENE 2

TIME: *One month later.*

SETTING: *Deserted saloon in a western ghost town. There is a bar at left piled high with barrels, and platform right for dancing girls. Round table stacked with overturned chairs is down left. Up right, a sign reading* DEADWOOD SALOON *dangles from broken chain over swinging doors.*

AT RISE: HENRY *peers over swinging door, then enters, shaking his head at desolate scene.* TWO-BITS *follows. They walk slowly, as if tired. They carry their coats and bundles over shoulders;* TWO-BITS *carries canteen.*

HENRY: Another ghost town. Must have been cleaned out by that bandit, Brute McGurk.

TWO-BITS: Sneaky old buzzard. He's picked the West clean, all right. Henry, I'm awfully tired — and I'm worried. Where are we going to get five thousand dollars before sundown tonight? (*Sound of approaching hoofbeats is heard.* HENRY *crosses to door and surveys scene outside.*)

HENRY: Somebody's coming! Somebody mean and ugly. Whew! He's wearing the worst-looking suit I ever saw.

TWO-BITS (*Pulling* HENRY *behind bar*): This is no time to be criticizing a suit, Henry. If he's that mean and ugly he must be Brute McGurk. Here he comes. Duck! (*They hide behind bar, watching action.* BRUTE MCGURK *and his henchmen* LOATHSOME TOAD *and* ONE-EYED JACK *enter through swinging door.*)

MCGURK (*Sniffing*): I smell gold. I smell it loud and strong.

TOAD: This here's a ghost town.

MCGURK (*Growling*): Are you disputin' the nose that knows? I tell you, I smell *gold* and I smell it *here*. Me

— McGurk with the educated sniffer! (*He sings to tune of "Captain Jinks."*)

    I'm Brute McGurk, the terrible Turk,

    I've many a strange and savage quirk —

    There's nothing I shirk like having to work —

    The meanest man in Nevada.

TOAD *and* JACK (*Singing*):

    He'd sell his grandma for a dime

    (McGURK *tosses a coin.*)

    Take baby's candy any time,

    Mow down a preacher in his prime

    (McGURK *shoots into air*)

    The meanest man in Nevada.

McGURK (*Singing and strutting*):

    I'm Brute McGurk come a-conquering,

    Riding to town for the golden ring,

    You can bet your boots I'll take anything —

    The meanest man in Nevada.

TOAD *and* JACK (*Singing*):

    He'll loot and shoot and steal and raid,

    A rootin', tootin' renegade,

    There's nothin' of which he is afraid —

TOAD (*Speaking*): He's the meanest, lowest, two-faced, lop-eared, beady-eyed, thick-skinned, yeller-dog, black-sheep, ringtailed-baboon skinna-marink scalawag —

TOAD *and* JACK (*Singing*):

    In Nevada!

TOAD: Brute McGurk. Nobody can outshoot you or out-smell you.

JACK: And you ain't afraid of anything or anybody!

McGURK: Yeah, yeah. Now get out. Scout around for the gold I keep smelling. (TOAD *and* JACK *exit.* McGURK

*glances back nervously over his shoulder, as if expecting
something. He crosses down center and speaks aside.*)
That wasn't exactly the gospel truth. I am afraid of
somebody . . . an ex-somebody. (HENRY *watches with
interest. Music to "Captain Jinks" is played slowly in
minor key.* MCGURK *sings to tune of "Captain Jinks."*)

When I was young I shot a man,
Shot off the pointer on his hand,
(*Holds up index finger*)
Said he, "I'll get you if I can,"
They called him — *Silverfinger.*

(*Speaking*) Silverfinger! The only man deadlier than I
am. Yes, I shot off his trigger finger and he never for-
gave me. He put a silver tip upon it to remind himself
how he hated me. I knew then I'd have to get him, before he got me . . . (*Singing*)

And though I galloped fast ahead,
To ambush *me* he swiftly sped,
But I bushwacked him, and shot him *dead* —
That devil, Silverfinger!

(*Speaking*) Yes, stone-cold dead. I got an engraved invitation to his funeral. There he was — all laid out like a
banker in a nice blue serge suit, holding a lily in the
hand with that cussed silver finger. Shucks, he can't
hurt me now. (*Peering over his shoulder, nervously*)
And yet (*Singing*) —

He cursed me, as he dying lay,
Said, "I'll come back one sunny day,
I'll come and spirit you away —
To the pit with Silverfinger!"

(*He looks over his shoulder again*) He's coming for me.
Don't know where or when, but one day I'll see the
sunbeams a-twinklin' on that silver fingertip, and I'll

be a goner. A goner! (*He glances over his shoulder as* TOAD *and* JACK *appear at doorway and whirls on them, with guns drawn.*) Who's there?

TOAD: Easy, boss, it's only us. Look what we found. (*They drag in* ANONYMOUS JONES *and dump him center.*)

JACK: It's that old coot, Anonymous Jones. The feller that was found half-dead on the beach near Frisco after that shipwreck years ago.

TOAD: He's going to tell us where the gold is, ain't you, Jones?

JONES (*Rising to knees, begging*): Water . . . water!

McGURK (*Shaking his canteen*): Here's the water — nice and cool. But first, tell us where the gold is.

JONES (*Shaking his head*): No gold here. Water, water!

JACK: Aw, he doesn't know anything.

McGURK: Where'd you find him?

TOAD: Up the creek. It's dry as a bone, but he was diggin' in the dust.

McGURK: Let's go. Maybe he was on to something up the creek.

JONES: Water . . .

McGURK (*Chuckling evilly*): You want water, old fool? (*Finishing water in his canteen*) I'll give you as much water as you gave me gold. (*He tosses empty canteen to* JONES, *who moans dismally*) Step over him and let's get out of here. (*They exit.* HENRY *and* TWO-BITS *rush from behind bar.* TWO-BITS *holds her canteen to* JONES'S *lips.*)

TWO-BITS: Here. Take our water. Oh, I never saw such meanness in all my born days!

JONES (*Feebly*): You mean — you'd give me your last drink of water?

HENRY: Of course we would. Drink hearty.

JONES (*Springing up, whacking* HENRY *on back with his hat*): You did it! You passed the test! You passed the Goodness and Kindness Test. By Neptune, I am proud to make you honorary citizens of this bee-yoo-tiful town. Welcome to Plentitude, Nevada, the Richest Town in the West. Shake hands with Mayor Jones! (*Extends his hand to* HENRY *and* TWO-BITS)

TWO-BITS (*Aside*): Poor old feller. He's gone plumb loco from the heat. (JONES *blows blast on bosun's whistle around his neck. Music to "Tavern in the Town" is heard.* HENRY *and* TWO-BITS *watch, amazed, as* TOWNS-FOLK, *in fancy clothes, and* COWBOYS, *in dressy rodeo outfits, enter from down left and right.* COWBOYS *and* TOWNSFOLK *slide away false walls left, right and up-stage, revealing elegant brocade walls hung with oil paintings and candle sconces. Barrels on bar are turned around to reveal shelves of books and sign reading* POETRY BAR. *Sign over doors is turned over and re-hung — it reads* PLENTITUDE, NEVADA *in gilt letters.* TOWNSFOLK *sit and stand around table down left, while* COWBOYS *stand at bar.* ANONYMOUS JONES *removes his tattered coat, revealing ruffled shirt and satin waistcoat. He exchanges battered captain's hat for top hat.*)

HENRY (*Rubbing his eyes*): It must be one of those mi-rages. This is a boom town! (*To* JONES) How'd you do it? How'd you get *so rich, so fast?*

JONES: Geography, matey.

TOWNSFOLK *and* COWBOYS: *Gee*-ogra-phy! (*Music of "Tavern in the Town" is heard.*)

JONES (*Singing to tune of "Tavern in the Town"*):
There is a gold mine 'neath the town,

TOWNSFOLK *and* COWBOYS (*Singing*):
  'Neath the town.
JONES (*Singing*):
  And silver, too, if you dig down,
TOWNSFOLK *and* COWBOYS (*Singing*):
  Just dig down,
JONES (*Singing; counting riches on his fingers*):
  And there's coal and oil and diamonds in the soil,
COWBOYS (*Singing*):
  And rubies for a rajah's crown!
TOWNSFOLK (*Singing*):
  Rajah's crown!
1ST WOMAN (*Singing*):
  Oh, the air is pure as glass is,
1ST MAN (*Singing*):
  And the soil rich as molasses,
2ND MAN (*Holding up mammoth ear of corn; singing*):
  You can grow an ear of corn from here to I-o-way.
JONES (*Singing*):
  Each citizen's a private king,
TOWNSFOLK *and* COWBOYS (*Singing*):
  Private king!
2ND WOMAN (*Holding up richly attired toy dog; singing*):
  Even dogs have everything,
TOWNSPEOPLE *and* COWBOYS (*Singing*):
  Everything,
JONES (*Singing*):
  We're so opulent we subsidize the mint,
  Wells Fargo comes three times a day!
TOWNSFOLK *and* COWBOYS (*Singing*):
  Every day!
  (WELLS FARGO MAN *enters as music continues with a vamp under conversation.*)

WELLS FARGO MAN: Mayor Jones, the East Coast respectfully requests a small cash advance of sixty million dollars.

JONES (*Pulling oversized check from pocket*): Take seventy
million.

WELLS FARGO MAN: Oh, thank you, sir. (*Bowing and
backing away*) Mr. Morgan thanks you. Mr. Carnegie
thanks you. Mr. Rockefeller thanks you. The entire
East Coast thanks you. (*Exits. Music stops.*)

TWO-BITS: Seventy million dollars! And that's only a drop
in the bucket. What do you do with all that money?
What could you possibly buy with all that cash?

JONES: Only one thing this town's in the market for. Only
one thing we can't get enough of. Culture!

COWBOYS *and* TOWNSFOLK: Culture! (*Sustained chord is
heard. Each singer sings following lines in recitative
fashion, beginning one note higher than previous singer,
until end of octave.*)

3RD WOMAN (*Singing*):
Plentitude, Nevada, has more culture in a tea cup
than Carson City has in a bucket . . .

3RD MAN (*Singing*):
Virginia City cannot hold a candle to our shining
light . . .

4TH WOMAN (*Singing*):
Even San Francisco takes a back seat to our fair
city . . .

4TH MAN (*Singing*):
Our salon is the equal of anything in Paris, France!

5TH WOMAN (*Singing*):
We have more books than the entire British Mu-
seum . . .

5TH MAN (*Singing*):
  More paintings than the Prado in Madrid . . .
6TH WOMAN (*Singing*):
  A better opera house than La Scala . . .
6TH MAN (*Singing*):
  The world's best dancing girls!
  (6TH MAN *brings out an easel with poster stating:* NOW!
  THE IMMORTAL ISADORA DUNCAN'S DELSARTE DANCERS.
  DELSARTE DANCERS, *in togas, scarves, and laurel
  wreaths, enter. Each carries Greek pillar which she sets
  up on platform. Florid arrangement of "Spring Song"
  is heard.* DANCERS *perform with scarves in style of
  Isadora Duncan. At finish all cheer.* DANCERS *exit.*)
4TH COWBOY (*Pounding on bar*): Open up the bar! Bring
  on the poetry! Where's the Bard Keeper?
COWBOYS (*Pounding; ad lib*): Bard Keeper! Bard Keeper!
  (BARD KEEPER *enters behind bar in frock coat, ascot
  and monocle. He carries feather duster.*)
BARD KEEPER: Keep your shirts on, gents. (*He dusts
  books.*) All right. The Poetry Bar is now open for business. Name your poison.
COWBOYS (*Shouting; ad lib*): Sonnets! Ballads! Rounde-
  lays! (*Etc.*)
1ST COWBOY: I'll stand everybody to a round of couplets.
  (*All* COWBOYS *cheer, except* 4TH COWBOY.)
BARD KEEPER (*Selecting book*): Couplets it is. Ahem. (*He
  declaims like an elocutionist.*)
    Early to bed, early to rise,
    Makes a man healthy, wealthy and wise.
4TH COWBOY: Doggerel!
1ST COWBOY: Did you call my couplet doggerel? Smile
  when you say that, pardner.
4TH COWBOY: You're cheap. Couplets — bah! I'll show

you how to treat a crowd. Bard Keeper, give us your best ode by Shelley.

BARD KEEPER: Aw, now, you know Shelley's too strong for you, Red. Why don't you have a nice little sonnet by Elizabeth Barrett Browning?

4TH COWBOY (*Pounding on bar*): I want Shelley! Gimme Shelley!

BARD KEEPER: Take him away, boys. He's on a Romantic bender again. Tsk-Tsk! I can smell Byron on his breath and it's only the middle of the afternoon. (2ND *and* 3RD COWBOYS *start to exit with* 4TH COWBOY.)

4TH COWBOY (*As he exits*): "Roll on, thou deep and dark blue ocean, roll!" (*He staggers offstage.*)

JONES (*To* HENRY): There it is, son. Plentitude, Nevada. The richest, most cultured town in the West. See why we have to hide it from sharks like Brute McGurk? We only let folks who pass the Goodness and Kindness Test stay here. When bad folks come along, we hide underground in the mine shafts, right underneath this salon. (*Burst of gunshots and shouting are heard from offstage.* WELLS FARGO MAN *enters center.*)

WELLS FARGO MAN: Lock up your silver and gold! Brute McGurk is coming! (*All ad lib consternation.*)

JONES: Anyone who wants to stay and fight — load your guns! (*All* TOWNSFOLK, COWBOYS, *and* BARD KEEPER *exit hurriedly, throwing guns on table.*) Say, isn't anybody going to stay and fight this hopeless battle? Five thousand dollars for anybody who'll stay and be sheriff! (*Sadly*) They've got plenty of culture, but they're a mite short on courage.

TWO-BITS: Did you say five thousand dollars? I'll stay and fight. (*She picks up two guns, holding them backward.*) Which end shoots, anyway?

HENRY: Put the guns down, Two-Bits. I accept your offer, Mr. Jones. I'll be your sheriff. I'll rid this town of Brute McGurk without telling a single lie or using a gun.

JONES (*In disbelief*): Get McGurk without a gun? I hope you have a will made out, matey! (*Shots and shouting offstage are heard again.*)

HENRY: You two get behind the pillars. I am going to show you how good tailoring can change a bad man. (TWO-BITS *and* JONES *hide.* HENRY *takes bandolier, tape, and scissors from bundle and dons them. He tucks flyswatter into belt. Then he crosses down right, and stands with his arms folded. In a moment* McGURK *swaggers onstage, and crosses center, looking over saloon.*)

McGURK: So, the ghost town ain't so ghostly after all! I knew this was a rich town. Stupid Jack and Toad, digging their hearts out, up the creek. (*He sniffs.*) My nose knew there was gold in this saloon. Thought they'd fool me, eh? (*He shoots into air.*) It's not nice to fool Brute McGurk! (*Spotting* HENRY) Why, it's a little gopher. Who're you?

HENRY: Afternoon, Mr. McGurk. I'm the new sheriff.

McGURK: You — a sheriff? Ha! I'll bet you think you've got me all sewed up.

HENRY: Not yet, Mr. McGurk. But I will have you all sewed up, very soon.

McGURK (*Threateningly*): Think you're tough, eh? How'd you like a cuff?

HENRY: How'd *you* like a cuff? You need cuffs more than I do.

McGURK: Why, you skinny little lizard, I could whip you with one hand!

HENRY: Maybe, but I could pin you good, and bind and lash you with no trouble at all. (*He dusts his hands and grins impishly at* MCGURK.)

MCGURK: Talk's cheap, gopher. Look. (*He crosses up center, sighting above swinging doors.*) See that dot in the sky? That's a buzzard a half mile off. Watch! (*He shoots. Slide whistle plays descending tone and there is a thump offstage.* MCGURK *points up proudly, looking offstage.*) One less buzzard.

HENRY (*Aside*): Lots of flies in this place. (*He swats with his hands, then hits his knee with a loud crack with flyswatter.*) Three! (MCGURK *turns quickly.*) Three with one shot.

MCGURK: Three varmints with one shot? (HENRY *nods.*) Dumb luck. Listen, gopher, I'll show you what shootin's all about. (*He crosses upstage again, sighting above doors.*) There's another buzzard. He's got a feather in his beak. I'll shoot the feather. (*He shoots. Slide whistle wavers as it descends. Sound of a tiny chime.* MCGURK *points offstage proudly.*) There. I never even touched the buzzard.

HENRY (*Brushing flies again, and cracking swatter on his other knee*): Seven! Seven with one shot! (MCGURK *crosses to* HENRY.)

MCGURK: Seven? You never got seven varmints with one shot!

HENRY: Sure I did. Want me to show you their totally dead bodies?

MCGURK: Never mind. (*Aside*) The gopher is quicker'n I thought. I'll have to get him before he gets me. (*To* HENRY) It's showdown time, gopher. Count off.

HENRY (*Taking tape from around his neck*): Count off? All right, if you say so. (*He measures* MCGURK'S *shoulders, chest and girth.*) Fifty-four — fifty-six — seventy-two. Whew! You'd best stop eating all those mashed potatoes, Mr. McGurk.

McGURK (*Crumpling up measuring tape*): Stop measuring me! There's only one thing a feller gets measured for — a pine box.

HENRY (*Scrutinizing* McGURK): Pine? Oh, I don't see you in pine. I was thinking of something more like — blue serge.

McGURK (*Rattled*): Blue serge? What made you think of blue serge? You make me nervous, gopher. (TWO-BITS *and* JONES *peer from behind pillars.*) Draw. (*He whips out his guns.*)

JONES (*Calling*): Run, matey! It's your only chance. (HENRY *pulls out his scissors, snapping them, as* McGURK *twirls his guns. They circle each other warily.*)

McGURK: I got you now, gopher. I'm going to fill you so full of holes they'll rinse noodles with you. (*He levels his guns at* HENRY.) One — two — (HENRY *grabs* McGURK's *suspenders, pulling them out like bowstrings.*)

HENRY (*Triumphantly*): Three! (*He cuts suspenders with a bold flourish of scissors.* McGURK *drops his guns and grabs for his trousers with one hand.*)

McGURK (*Dismayed, then furious*): My guns! You made me drop my guns! I never dropped my guns for no man! (*He grabs* HENRY *in a fierce bear hug around neck.*) You sneakin' varmint! I'll show you what we do with gophers out here in the West. We *squash* 'em!

HENRY (*Gasping*): Let go, Mr. McGurk! You're poppin' all your buttons. (*He digs into his pocket, puts thimble on his finger and waves it desperately in* McGURK's *face.*)

McGURK: What's that on your finger? (*He releases* HENRY *and backs away terrified.*) What's that twinklin' in the sunbeams? No! Don't haunt me! Leave me be, Silverfinger! (HENRY *smiles and wags his finger.* McGURK *covers his eyes and goes down on his knees.*) Don't torture me! I'll do anything for you!

HENRY: Will you go far away and leave honest folks alone?

McGURK: Yes, yes. Can I go now?

HENRY: Nope. You have to forsake your guns.

McGURK: They're forsaken. Can I go now? Please, Silverfinger?

HENRY: Nope. You have to take up an honest trade — like delivering milk.

McGURK: Deliver milk? Aw, have a heart. (HENRY *waves thimble.*) I'll do it. Can I go *now?*

HENRY: Throw your guns on the table. (McGURK *picks up guns and puts them on table.*) You can go now. (McGURK *hurriedly crosses up center.*) Oh, one more thing, Mr. McGurk.

McGURK: Anything. Anything.

HENRY: Get yourself a new suit.

McGURK (*Bowing and scraping*): Oh, yes, sir, Silverfinger. I will. I certainly will. (*He exits. Sound of receding hoofbeats is heard offstage.* TWO-BITS *and* JONES *cross to* HENRY, *jubilant.*)

JONES: By the great hornspoon, you did it, lad. (*Pulling out money from his pocket*) Here's my payment in full — five thousand dollars. (*He hands money to* HENRY.)

TWO-BITS (*Embracing* HENRY): Oh, Henry, you've saved the Cozy home! (*Sound of small bell tinkling is heard.* JONES *clutches his head, staring out into space.*)

JONES: I heard a little bell a-tinkling far off. What was

that you said about a home, Missy?

TWO-BITS: Why, the orphan home. Henry's got five thousand dollars to pay off the mortgage on Ma Cozy's orphan home. We've got to leave here now, before sundown. (*Sound of large bell is heard.*)

JONES: That bell is getting louder. Did you say — Ma Cozy? Is she a nice round little woman, always cries a lot when she's happy?

HENRY: That's our Ma Cozy. Mrs. Amelia Cozy. Know her? (*Sound of large bell tolling*)

JONES: Ding-Dong! Amelia Cozy. It's all coming back, like the tide. Amelia Cozy is my long-lost wife.

TWO-BITS *and* HENRY (*Together*): Then you must be her long-lost husband (*Dramatic chord is played.*) — Captain Barney Cozy!

JONES: Barney Cozy. That's me. Why, I ain't Anonymous at all! By the great hornspoon, I've found myself!

HENRY: Come home with us, Captain Cozy.

JONES: What are we waitin' for? Hoist up the anchor and full speed ahead! We'll take the Wells Fargo wagon! (*Chorus of "Seeing Nellie Home" is played in spritely manner.*)

TWO-BITS, HENRY *and* JONES (*Singing to tune of "Seeing Nellie Home"*):
We will save our Cozy home,
Yes, we'll save our Cozy home,

JONES (*Singing*):
Get those wheels a-hummin' — rescue's comin'!

TWO-BITS, HENRY *and* JONES (*Singing*):
Saving our Cozy home!

(*Curtain. Reprise of songs is played while scene is changed.*)

* * * * *

Scene 3

Time: *Later that night.*

Setting: *Same as Scene 1.*

At Rise: Ma Cozy *is seated in rocker, darning socks and singing.* Annie *and* Oliver *enter in nightclothes, rubbing their eyes and yawning. They sit at her feet.*

Ma Cozy (*Singing to tune of "My Bonnie Lies Over the Ocean"*):

My Barney sailed over the ocean,
Far over the deep, stormy sea,
He never returned to his harbor.
Oh, where can my poor Barney be?

Bring back, bring back,
Oh, bring back my Barney to me, to me,
Bring back, bring back,
Oh, bring back my Barney to me.

(*Speaks*) Annie — Oliver. You should be in bed. It's almost midnight.

Annie: We couldn't sleep.

Oliver: We were worried about Henry and Two-Bits. Do you think they'll ever come back?

Ma Cozy: Now, now, children. This is only the twenty-eighth day of the month. There's still plenty of time. (*Chimes begin to sound*) Listen — it's midnight. (*Thundering knock is heard.*)

Annie *and* Oliver (*Together*): They've come home! (*They run to open door.* Lawyer Grudge *bounds in, sneering.*)

Ma Cozy: Lawyer Grudge!

Grudge: Why so surprised, madam? I have come at the proper time. The stroke of midnight at the passing of the old month.

MA COZY: Sir, you are mistaken. This is but the twenty-eighth day.

GRUDGE: The twenty-eighth day of *February*.

MA COZY: Oh-h. *February*.

GRUDGE: And now, 'tis March — a new month. Pack up your orphans, Mrs. Cozy, and vacate these premises. (MA COZY *puts her arms around* ANNIE *and* OLIVER *protectively as they begin to wail.*)

TWO-BITS, HENRY *and* JONES (*Offstage; singing cheerily*): We will save our Cozy home . . . (*Etc.*)

ANNIE: Listen!

OLIVER: They're here! We're saved! (*They rush to open door.* HENRY, TWO-BITS *and* JONES *enter.*)

MA COZY: Oh, I knew you'd come in time. Welcome home, Henry and Two-Bits, and (*To* JONES) — and you too, stranger.

HENRY: We took the Wells Fargo wagon lickety-split straight here. We didn't even stop to visit the Grand Canyon.

TWO-BITS (*Waving packet of money*): And we've got the five thousand dollars in a tidy bundle. Just the way we promised.

HENRY: But best of all, we've brought you — him! (*Pointing to* JONES)

JONES (*To* MA COZY): Amelia! (*He holds out his arms. Sound of small bell tinkling is heard.*)

MA COZY: I know that voice.

JONES (*Coming closer*): Look close. Don't you remember me? (*Sound of larger bell ringing*)

MA COZY: I've seen that face.

JONES: Ahoy, Amelia! Your own true love has reached his snug harbor at last. (*Sound of bells pealing is heard as they embrace.*)

MA COZY: Barney! My long-lost and late-lamented Barney! (ANNIE *and* OLIVER *cheer.*)

GRUDGE (*Sneering*): A pretty sight, but you're too late. This place is mine.

JONES: Lawyer Grudge! Why, you surly shark, what are you doing in my house? Begone!

GRUDGE: Fools! The chimes have rung in a new month. You did not come forward with the money at the time I specified. Now you must forfeit your home. (*He waves a document.*) This document says so.

TWO-BITS: We won't go, you old prune.

GRUDGE: Don't sass me, you little snip. This legal paper's powerful.

TWO-BITS: Paper's nothing. It's people that count. (*She takes torn scrap of parchment from her pocket and waves it under* GRUDGE*'s nose.*) I could wave a paper at you too, but it doesn't mean one thing. (GRUDGE *snatches paper, examines it, then looks up, startled. Dramatic chord is played.*)

GRUDGE: Can this be what I think it is? (*He matches scrap with piece of parchment he takes from waistcoat pocket, holding them up so audience can see they match.*) It is! The Grudge family coat of arms — cashboxes rampant on a field of gold coins. Where did you find this, girl? Only my nephew Ralph had this coat of arms.

TWO-BITS: It was pinned to my raggedy pink blanket when I was found in a basket on the steps of this very home.

GRUDGE (*Aside*): Dare I hope? I must test her to find out for sure if she is the heir to the Grudge fortune. (*He advances toward* TWO-BITS *as others watch anxiously.*) What is your favorite motto, child?

TWO-BITS: Waste not, want not. (GRUDGE *comes closer.*)

GRUDGE: If I gave you a copper coin, what would you do with it?

TWO-BITS: Put it in a sock under my mattress, of course. (GRUDGE *comes closer.*)

GRUDGE: You could have guessed those answers. There is one final test. What flashes into your mind when I speak these words: Trust —

TWO-BITS: Beneficiary!

GRUDGE (*Excited*): Real —

TWO-BITS: Estate!

GRUDGE: Satisfaction —

TWO-BITS: Cash! (*Fanfare is heard.*)

GRUDGE: You said the magic word. You are a true Grudge. Niece! All that I have is yours.

TWO-BITS (*Embracing him*): Uncle! I'll take it. (NICHOLAS, EM, DAVEY *and* NELL *rush onstage. They have a joyous reunion with* TWO-BITS *and* HENRY.)

GRUDGE (*Rubbing his hands together*): And now, I have a little bit of unfinished business . . .

TWO-BITS: Uncle Grudge, if you put my friends out in the snow, you can say goodbye to me.

GRUDGE: Would you give up a fortune for (*Waving arm around room; in disbelief*) this?

TWO-BITS: I certainly would. Take me or leave me! (*She crosses upstage toward exit as all cheer.*)

GRUDGE (*Reluctantly*): I'll — I'll take you! (*He tears up document.*)

OLIVER: Hurrah for Uncle Grudge!

OTHER ORPHANS: Hurrah for Uncle Grudge!

GRUDGE (*Wincing*): Bah! I hate little children! Don't any of you ask to be bounced on my knee. Curses! (HENRY *takes* TWO-BITS *by the hand and crosses down center with her.*)

HENRY: By golly, Two-Bits, you are something special. Why, you just skunked the meanest man in the East.

TWO-BITS: Shucks, Henry. It was nothing compared to you. You skunked the meanest man in the West.

HENRY: Two-Bits, you know what?

TWO-BITS: What, Henry?

HENRY: Ma Cozy said I shouldn't lie, cuss, drink distilled spirits or shoot a gun.

TWO-BITS: That's right, Henry, she did.

HENRY (*Grinning broadly*): But she didn't say a word about this! (*Gives her a kiss*)

TWO-BITS (*Breaking into broad grin*): That's right, Henry. She sure didn't! (*Gives him a kiss; all cheer. Music to "Seeing Nellie Home" begins. All form tableau with* TWO-BITS *and* HENRY *at center, and sing finale.*)

ALL (*Singing to tune of "Seeing Nellie Home"*):
> We have saved our Cozy home,
> Yes, we've saved our Cozy home,
> Now we'll all live happily ever after —

GRUDGE (*Speaking*): Curses!

ALL (*Singing*):
> Here in our Cozy home. (*Repeating*)
> Here — in — our — Cozy — home!

(*Curtain*)

THE END

The Fastest Thimble in the West

PRODUCTION NOTES

Characters: 15 female; 21 male. (Parts may be doubled or extra Townsfolk, Cowboys and Dancers may be added if desired.)

Playing Time: 45 minutes.

Costumes: Ma Cozy, house gown, apron, white hair, spectacles. Two-Bits, gown and apron, cloak. Henry, early 1900s style suit, coat. Orphans, night-clothes. Girl orphans wear hair in rag curls. Lawyer Grudge, black suit, cape, top hat, moustache. Anonymous Jones, dusty, baggy outer clothes, shapeless Captain's hat, bosun's whistle, satin waistcoat, ruffled shirt, top hat. Wells Fargo man, uniform cap lettered WELLS FARGO, blue uniform. Brute McGurk, ill-fitting jeans, ragged shirt, wide suspenders, prop gun with caps or blanks, canteen, boots, stubbly beard, sheepskin bolero, bullet-riddled sombrero, bandolier. One-Eyed Jack, eye patch, black stetson, black, ill-fitting suit, boots. Loathsome Toad, chaps, boots, badly patched shirt, shoulder-slung rifle, battered fedora. Delsarte dancers, white togas, ballet slippers, wreaths, scarves. Townsfolk, "swell" clothes of the period. Cowboys, satin shirts, chaps sewn with sparklers, bright neckerchieves, prop guns. Bard Keeper, frock coat, black ascot, top hat. Extra coat and top hat for Oliver.

Properties: Fire poker; firescreen; portrait; candle; coat rack; umbrella stand; hobo bundles; brush; rag; tailor's dummy; sewing basket; tea table; pitcher; mugs; marshmallows; washbasket with pink blanket; prop snow; needle and thread; small scissors; document; quill pen; two torn papers (Grudge and Two-Bits); measuring tape; bandolier of thread; scissors in holster; silver thimble; sequinned flyswatter; barrels; sign; chairs; table; coin; prop guns; canteens; bosun's whistle; books; pillars; mammoth ear of corn; stuffed poodle in robe and crown; outsized checks; sock; darning egg; easel and poster reading NOW! THE IMMORTAL ISADORA DUNCAN'S DELSARTE DANCERS; feather duster; money.

Setting: The same basic box set may be used for both scenes. There are exits up right, up left, down right and down left. Scene 1 is a living room interior with fireplace up left, window right, outside door up left. There are wing chairs up left and right beside fireplace, and rocker down right. Above mantel is portrait of Captain Barney Cozy, Ma Cozy's long-lost sea-captain husband. On wall is sampler reading MA COZY'S HOME FOR HAPPY ORPHANS. Next to door up right stands coat rack, holding coats for Two-Bits and Henry, and umbrella stand with two hobo bundles and flyswatter. There is candle on windowsill. Scene 2: Curtains open on deserted saloon. Swinging doors are up right. Sign reading DEADWOOD SALOON dangles from broken chain over doors. There is a platform right for dancing girls. There is a round table stacked with chairs down left. There is a bar at right, piled with barrels. At the signal from Anonymous Jones, actors quickly slide away or take down false walls, revealing walls with brocade wallpaper, oil paintings and candle sconces, giving room look of elegant salon. Dancers set up four Greek pillars on platform to add to the effect of Culture.

Lighting: No special effects.

Sound: Whistling wind, knocking, hoofbeats approaching and retreating, gun-shots, slide whistle effects, graduated bells (tinkling, ringing, gonging, pealing), real or on records, and chimes, as indicated in text. The music may be played by piano, or by western band with guitars, banjo, mandolin, harmonica, etc. Jug band may entertain during intermissions. Musical punctuation consisting of dramatic chords or "stings," vamps, fanfares, and chords adds to the pace of the performance and may be performed by piano or band. If desired, recorded music may accompany songs.